1

Buttermilk Book Publishing

Myrtle Beach, South Carolina

The story and characters are the work of a lifetime of playing golf.
All is for good fun and entertainment, a tongue in cheek approach to
the so-called gentleman's game.

Typecast in Times New Roman

ISBN 978-1-7331576-0-5

The Endless Mulligan

Short Shots from the Golf Whomper

I'm stumped…time for a foot wedge!

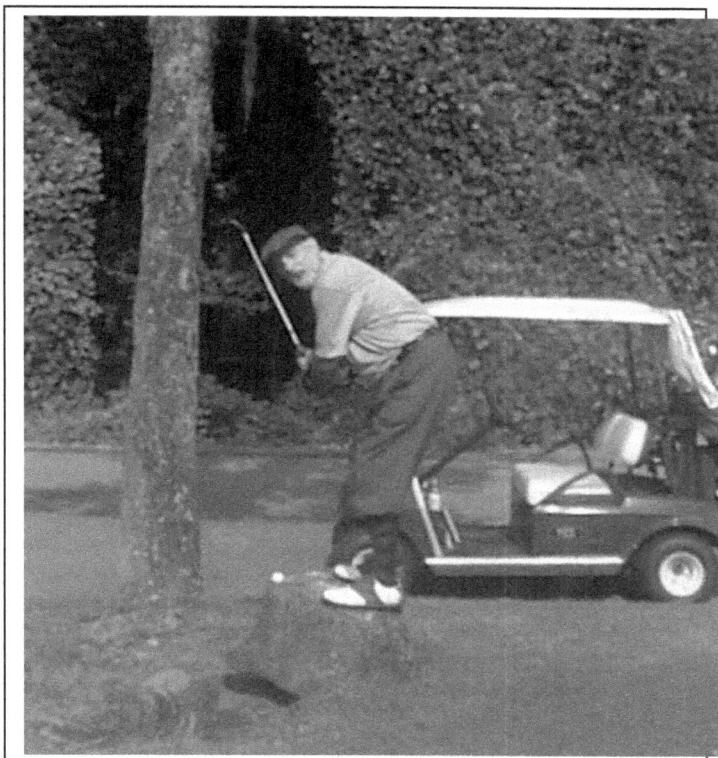

'Fore' Word

I've accumulated these golf short stories for more years than I dare count. I sincerely hope that those who supplied the fodder appreciate the tongue and cheek approach to the story telling. I have been the source of many of these outings as well. Sometimes I have excluded names. Other times I have included the names of my partners in crime on the links. All meant for fun reading, making sport of myself as well as of my assortment of playing partners and unique situations. Life's lessons learned. While the theme is based on golf, look beyond the episodes and embrace the journey. Personalities and personal quirkiness tend to float to the surface during a friendly round of golf fellowship. I have met and made many new friends on the numerous courses I have played. Most have been memorable and too often they have been unforgettable. From the courses located in the South Carolina upstate, Greenwood, Abbeville and McCormick counties to where I reside in retirement bliss on the South Carolina Grand Strand, a round is usually sprinkled with all sorts of challenges. The course layout, the various hazards and even the local animal population can play intricate roles in a round.

And then there are the rules associated with playing what some depict as the gentleman's game. For what it is worth, rules are extremely overrated, and gentlemen are seldom found in the golf circuit of my Whomper World. We adjust the rules when appropriate. It takes all kinds to form a foursome. As for the term, Whomper, you'll experience that journey in the opening short shot. Even if you have never graced a driving range, a putting green, tee box or fairway, you'll enjoy this lighthearted approach to a game not meant for some to play. That hasn't stopped us from trying though. Perhaps some of us should have left well enough alone. Maybe we should have limited our play to miniature golf or as some call it, putt-putt. Windmills, dinosaurs and an assortment of iconic obstacles are challenging enough for most of us. You really don't need a driver to send a ball out of bounds on these whimsical wonderlands. A venue supplied putter is enough for most of these miniature theme lands.

I'd like to acknowledge Abbeville's Flexible Technologies third shift crew that introduced me to the gentleman's game one morning in the mid 70's at the High Meadows nine-hole course. There the course birthed the legendary Whomper. And a special thank you goes out to Greenwood's Kemet Wednesday Whomper's League of the late 90's-early 2000 timeframe. Golf Hound was our official scorer for the group. Friends, family and strangers have made my life in golf an interesting journey as I'm sure I have had the same impact on those who have had the pleasure of sharing a round with me. Friendships know no boundaries, playing with folks in Clover, S.C. and in Commerce, Georgia during my life as a quality systems consultant. And, then there are those who took me in under their wings at Metglas, Inc. in Conway in Horry County after we moved to Myrtle Beach in 2005. And if you feel I have excluded you, just wait, you might just be in the short shots within the following pages. Buckle up, bring extra golf balls and an ample supply of do-overs. Keeping score is optional but the game begins now.

Golf is deceptively simple and endlessly complicated; it satisfies the soul and frustrates the intellect. It is at the same time rewarding and maddening - and it is without a doubt the greatest game mankind has ever invented.
Arnold Palmer

Short Shots by the Chapters

What is to Whomp?

Gauging a Good Round

Hazardous Play

Hitting My Woods

Strategy, So Overrated

Greenhorns

Closest to the Pin

I Get No Respect

Nature's Wondrous Waterways

The Flim-Flam Man

Raspberries and Rulings

Score Card Rules

Scoring 95, Shooting 106

My Cheap Golf Date

The Darnedest Things

The 19th Hole of Horror

Look Good, Feel Good, Play Good and Smell Good

The Coon Whisperer

The State Bird

Mother Nature's Wild Kingdom

Be Berry, Berry Quiet, We're Hunting Gators

The Golf Planner

The Golfer's Kitchen Pass

Blame it on Ken

O.C. Call Home

Calling Sigmund Freud

La-La Land

Hey Mr. Ranger, Where's Yogi?

Golfing with a Southern Belle

The Golf Streak

Octogenarians

Here's Johnny

Rockin' Ronny

The Wise Guy

License to Kill

Incoming

The Swiss Army Machete

Cold Beer

The Category One

Lightning up the Course

Double Secret Probation

Totally Eclipsed at Tupelo Bay

Scuba-Duba-Do, Where Are You?

Masters of the Game

There's No Place Like Gnome

Rope-a-Dope, Float like a Butterfly, Sting like a Bee

All Aboard the Crazy Train

Snowbirds and Seagulls

Shoeless Joe Jackson

If My Papa John Bowie Had Played Golf

The Immortal

The Cousin Memorial Outing

3rd Annual Cousins, In-laws, Outlaws and Branch Kin Golf Tournament

The Endless Mulligan, the Art of the Do-Over

What is to *Whomp*?

Whomp is probably not a golfing term familiar to most. Duffer or hacker is probably a more popular name tag reserved for those who lack the expertise to excel at the sport designated for gentlemen. I had never considered playing the game and seldom watched golf tournaments on television as a kid or young adult. I'm sure you're questioning what qualifies me to pen a book about golf. You certainly have the right to your opinion. Let's continue the round just the same. I'm not suggesting you might pick up some helpful tips, but you could have a few belly laughs. Sit back and experience the game from the perspective of someone who was never supposed to play the game. For the record, I am the original Whomper so who better to provide an explanation and *Whomping* lesson. You've all probably *Whomped* a time or two in your golfing career. You just didn't recognize your attempt to strike a ball as a *Whomp*. Let us begin by defining the origin of the Whomp.

Spring of 1973, as a young man just starting my tour of duty in the working world, I had never envisioned myself on the links. Working the third shift or midnight shift as most dub it, the boys were always looking for group activities to promote male bonding. Finishing our shift at 7:30 AM, we had already tried tennis, bowling and trail bike riding to mention a few. We embraced the challenges, something to quench our desire to conquer the next greatest thing. Why not try golf? My associates all owned a set of clubs. I didn't. They encouraged me to tag along one morning after work at High Meadows Country Club, a nine-hole local course between my hometown of Abbeville and Lownsville, South Carolina. They offered me the use of their clubs. I could choose between a righthanded and lefthanded set. How was I supposed to know if I hit the ball left or right? I thought hitting it straight was the premise of the game. Okay. I get it. I am a righty. Selection made. They even supplied the balls, an expensive decision for them. I didn't realize that the balls came in such a variety of brands, not that it would impact my ability to play the game.

Lesson #1, you should never take your first golf lesson on the course. Lesson #2, go home, sleep first and then play when refreshed. Lesson #3, stick with bowling where high scores are a good thing. Lesson #4, golf balls are purchased in multiple quantities because you're not expected to play with the same ball for extended periods. Lesson #5, it isn't really that easy to hit a stationary object.

On the first tee I learned the term, whiff, and that it equated to side and back pain. They advised, "Slow down your back swing." They didn't tell me what to do with my front swing. They encouraged me to keep my eye on the ball. That worked. Now I could see where the ball was after I whiffed. Keeping my eye fixated on the ball resting atop that tee did nothing to slow my back swing. Harder isn't better though, especially if you fail to make contact with the ball.

Abandoning my windmill technique, I finally overcame the whiff on the first tee box after about five or six swings. My buddies lent bits of encouragement telling me that those missed swings didn't count and I was getting closer with my misses. Practice in my case didn't' build on perfection. Executing my version of a fast 'slower' swing I finally made first contact. I then realized my natural ability to worm burn after a few simple adjustments. Worm burners are a lot better than whiffs, especially if they go straight and there is no water ahead, Mine didn't and yes, I found every drop of water that day. I think I even hit the water cooler. But, improvements, even marginal, are part of the learning curve, right? Finally, off the tee box, it was a pleasant change of scenery. I'm sure my instructors were relieved that we were advancing our agenda. Our night shift would be here before you know it at this pace.

For my first fairway shot, they handed me a three wood; whiff then *Whomp*! Second, third, forth, fifth and sixth fairway shots, *Whomp, Whomp, Whomp, Whomp* and *Whomped* it again. I recall they stopped counting my strokes on the par four somewhere after those *whomps* reached double digits. Same drill on the next tee box, whiffing, worm burning and whomping numerous times. I had found a tempo. That theme played out over the next several holes, but the ball finally went places, a lot of places. Riding one of those electric carts would have been better than walking and pulling the bags on carts like we were doing. We were young and broke or maybe just cheap.

Finally, on number six, one of my cohorts, after consuming mass quantities of adult beverages (the breakfast of third shift champions), yelled, "*Whomp* it, come on, *Whomp* it again!"

Another cheerleader echoed the first, "Hit it, *Whomp*. You can do it, *Whomp*!" Apparently, evolution had kicked in as I no longer just *whomped the golf ball*. I had acquired my new nick name, *Whomp*.

You're still not with me, are you? Let's bring in Mister Webster. Maybe he can help. Definitions applicable to *Whomp*: (1) A loud, heavy blow or thud (2) To hit or strike (3) hit with something flat, like a paddle or the open hand (4) strike somebody or something. When I attempted to strike the ball, I *whomped* the ground first. I guess the club served as my paddle contributing to the distinctive sound. That covers definition one through three.

I secured definition number four on the par four ninth fairway. Dale 'Beulah' McCurry, a rather big boned, healthy young man, happened to be standing in the middle of the fairway with his pull cart about a hundred yards ahead of me. He motioned for me to go ahead and hit the ball figuring I had not hit a fairway all day. Center of the fairway seemed to be the safest place. Bad decision. I nailed a straight as an arrow line drive that *Whomped* him in his left shoulder as he tried to duck behind his pull car. It dropped him to his knees. He sure ruined my best shot. It careened out of the fairway into the trees, a familiar place for me.

Dale 'Beulah' McCurry and Me
'Rest in Peace My Friend'

Over the years I've managed to hold on to that name, *Whomp* or *Whomper*. Heck, I even founded the WGA (Whomper Golf Association). One of my latter work groups dubbed the Wednesday *Whompers* had an annual Whomper Classic. One member even provided a sleeve of balls and tees during our last outing with Wednesday *Whompers* printed on them. We eventually all went our separate ways but still managed that annual Whomper reunion where we played a nine-hole par three course, a nine-hole executive course, before breaking for lunch and then finishing on our regulation nine-hole course. We did plenty of *Whomping* on those Saturdays.

I live on the Grand Strand now. While the beach golfers I presently partner up with are much improved over my former companions, I still find myself referring to us as *Whompers*. Once a *Whomper*, always a *Whomper* as I proved by shooting my all time low of 89 at Arrowhead golf course and then followed that a week later with 124 at the same course. I convinced myself that I needed the 124 to re-qualify my WGA card before our next reunion. I still suck at the game but do enjoy *Whomping* that ball. I just try not to play with serious golfers because they don't appreciate my natural abilities.

"Yawl *whomp'em* good out there, you hear?"

Gauging a Good Round

I never judge my round of whomping the ball by the number of strokes it took me to complete it. I'm way too laid back to be stressed out over a golf score. Golfers beware, playing a round with me is not recommended for the serious or strategic golfer. I'm not a score card watcher. Typically, I have no clue what I shot until each nine has been tallied. I keep score most of the time for the group and it doesn't affect me no matter how good or bad I am shooting. I take it one hole at a time, and it is what it is. Now don't get me wrong. I do hate to shoot badly but most of the time I refuse to allow it to ruin my day. Let's put this in perspective though. This mantra was mine in my early career of whomping. With improvement, expectations evolve. Patience gives way to spurts of impatience. Imperfection seeks glimpses of perfection, marginally at best, but measurable. I try my best to not allow my perturbed state to interfere with those playing much better. Here's how I judge my round.

If I finished with more balls than I started or played with the same balls the entire round, I have just completed a good round. I have a knack for finding other people's lost balls. It may have something to do with me venturing off the fairway in search and rescue mode for my own. Most golfers will not go where most balls have never gone before. Briars, poison ivy and snakes are deterrents in the Carolina upstate. Toss in alligators along the coast. Snake chaps and gator equalizers usually aren't items kept in golf bags.

If I escaped the *dirt*, aka the sand traps in one shot, I had a good round. Or better still, I hit into no bunkers, strokes were probably saved. I love the beach but playing in the sand just isn't the same without a pale and shovel. A shovel might be a better choice than a sand wedge in my play.

If I successfully got off the first tee box, then I am excited about my potential round. Saving face in front of a crowd is a good thing. My goal is to just hit it somewhere, hopefully with a bit of distance between me and where it landed. Forward and pass the lady's tee box is considered a monumental achievement.

If I hit my fairway shots long, and again anywhere, I have had a good round. Far for me means I made contact and I don't always make great contact. I don't whiff it as much as I used to, but I can still pull off a masterful whomp or worm burner. Direction is highly overrated and hinges on strategy. I don't do strategy. My strategy is simple. If all works well, the ball goes somewhere. Hopefully I find it and I have a shot to hit it to a new location. Gauging the distance to hit the next shot or deciding on a direction to hit it is over the top strategically for my game. Eventually, I'll make it to the green or I won't. Double pars just mean I practiced more.

If it doesn't rain before or during the round, or I have an early tee time absent of morning dew, then I have had a good round. I don't do wet well. For whatever reason, it tends to just mentally mess with me. The 90-degree rule trumps 'cart path only' every time!

Water hazards are wet so clearing those makes for a good round even if I shoot an eight on the hole. Did I mention that I hate wet?

Avoiding double par or those dreaded evil snowmen makes for a great round of golf. For you non golfers, a snowman is an eight on your score card. A natural six on a par three is acceptable. I often claim triples because that sounds better than declaring a double par. Picking up your ball after double par works for me if your foursome allows you to do so. Most do. It speeds up the already slow round.

We allow one mulligan every nine holes of play. A mulligan is an extra shot claimed after a bad shot made. Having a mulligan left on the final hole equates to a good round, unless I've had too many opportunities to apply it and just didn't.

Not being tossed from the golf cart by the cart's driver lends to having a good round of golf. I have been thrown from carts before when the designated driver, for whatever reason, decided to make one of those hard-left maneuvers. I've been raked from the cart when my cart buddy drove through low hanging limbs on my side of the cart of course. I prohibit certain golfing buds from ever driving a cart if I'm the passenger, instructing the attendant to place their bag on the right side, securing them in the shotgun seat.

Keeping the round moving always makes for a good round of golf. The kiss of death for me is waiting too long for the group ahead or having the OC boys playing in my group. Obsessive Compulsive behavior can grind a round to a stop. We do have two anal retentive gentlemen in our Grand Strand group. Candy wrappers or cigarette butts on the fairways drives one of them totally crazy. We'll leave that for another tale though.

I've had a good round if my teammates have managed to complete eighteen holes without feuding among themselves or have not picked a fight with the group ahead or behind us. Adult beverages may or may not play a role in these altercations.

If I have completed eighteen holes before dark-thirty then I have had a good round. To strike the ball and listen for it to land technique is not very effective when darkness has slammed the door on your round. I've seen some of my playing partners' best rounds ruined on that last hole when they've either lost their ball or can't judge the distance or direction to hit it. Not seeing where I have whomped the ball isn't necessarily bad for my game. Remember, I hit the ball and hopefully I get to hit it again, if I can find it.

Any round among friends is better than no round at all. Heck, a round with mortal enemies is a good round most of the time. Try not to raise the bar too high because I can almost certainly guarantee you will be sadly disappointed. If you're not achieving your goal, then lower your expectations. The game takes no prisoners. Survive the best way you can, and you too can boast you have had a good round. It's a game. Play it like one and have fun.

Hazardous Play

Hazards can slam you when you least expect it. These are not always adequately defined so I will expand on this by providing you with the *Whomper's Guide to Hazards and How to Play Them.*

Water hazards: Make a sacrifice and toss a ball into the water before your hit your shot. Appeasing the Water gods can't hurt. Or, strategically skip your ball across the surface. Yes, your ball can walk on the water and can sometimes make it to the other side. Always keep one of those telescopic ball retrievers in your golf bag. Swimming pools qualify as a water hazard. Yes, I have hit my ball into a pool. I cut the dogleg a bit too much once on the Heritage course in Pawley's Island. While searching for my ball, a young lady shouted out to me from where she and three others were sitting at a table under a colorful umbrella. She asked if I was looking for my ball. I nodded yes. She confirmed it was in the swimming pool. A guy in the group advised that I take a drop, no penalty. The two couples were very accommodating considering.

Bunkers: That fluffy white sand is not your friend. You must learn the proper technique to escape its clutches. Wet sand is evil reincarnate and can ruin a good score or round. Pot bunkers, good luck. You're on your own. It may be a good time to make another one of those sacrifices. The dreaded ball against the trap's lip shot; just pencil in a double par on the score card.

The environmentally sensitive areas: These are usually marked with a sign to prevent entry. You really don't want to risk entering them anyway, unless you're wearing snake chaps. They can often be creature infested swamps and bogs. I refer to them as environmentally unfriendly to my play. Take your penalty. Drop a ball on the other side. There is no need going 'tin cup' just to prove you can sail across the forbidden zone. Balls are not cheap.

Pine needles and pinecones: Hate'em, can't play'em and costs me several strokes to reach a fairway, any fairway. Exercise a foot wedge if possible. Kick the ball onto a grassy spot every opportunity you get. Torch the area on your way out.

Rock and Root forever: Never strike a ball on tree roots or rocks unless you have no choice because of tournament or league play. One, it can damage your club and two, it can damage you. Foot wedge it to improve the lie and make sure you fluff up your new location when repositioning the ball.

Rakes: Move all of them out of your direct path. You never know when you're going to hit that worm burner or ricochet into the bunker. If a rake is protecting the bunker, leave it there as it may protect you from entering the sandy abyss. Claim a 'do-over' if the rake lands you in a perilous position.

Condos, town houses and houses: stupid place for them along a golf course. Before hitting your tee shot, yell, "Get the women and small children inside." If you are unlucky and hit one, remember this important ploy. If the resident didn't see who hit the ball, point to your playing partner. He or she is then on defense. Convincing the homeowner that they are innocent is nearly impossible once blame has been designated. Plan B, when retrieving your ball; always yell back at your cart buddy, "I found your ball!" If you break a window, just haul ass. Every person for themself.

Natural areas: Avoid hitting from flowers and shrubs or places where those little ornamental elves are standing, unless you are sure no one is at home and it'll ensure that you at least make a double boggy.

Bird houses and Club houses: Claim a do-over because they shouldn't put them where you're trying to hit.

Other fairways: That's why they are called fair. Forget those club rules about out of bounds and play your shot after that other foursome plays through. Hopefully it will offer a shortcut. If not, it's only a game, right?

Tee Markers: If you hit yours then you should not be on a golf course. If you hit the ones ahead of you, call the do-over. Of course, you know the rule for not getting pass the women's tee box. Your pals will say that you must whip it out. Hope you are anatomically correct, or your buddies might just nickname you Peewee or worse, Peewee wantabee!

Ball washers: Hit one, retrieve your ball and use the washer to clean it. Replace the ball in the fairway and don't include that stroke in your final tally. Or declare a do-over. By the time you hole out your partners will have forgotten about it hopefully.

Cart paths: Roll of the dice here. It can launch your ball into the abyss never to be seen again or it may provide you with the longest drive of your life. Friend or foe, you'll know after the ball stops rolling or bouncing. If your ball comes to rest on the cart path, then exercise the foot wedge. There is no limit on the number of foot wedges during a round.

Carts: My experience, always park them behind you. I've hit too many parked either ahead or directly to my right or left. Embarrassing take you medicine and move on.

Playing Partners: Same as above applies. Just pray you didn't kill him or warrant a hospital stay.

Ditches: Man made areas so drop your ball out improving and fluffing the lie and never count a penalty stroke. Foot wedges permitted.

Curbing: Move the ball one club length and don't count a penalty stroke. Remember to fluff it up though. There's no need wasting a ball placement. Take whatever advantages your playing partners will allow. Trust me. They'll let you know if you have taken too many liberties.

Gators: Consider all the possibilities if your ball comes to rest within chomping distance of an alligator. How lucky do you feel? How much adult beverages have you consumed? Did your buddies

26

dare you? Is this a Kodak moment? How quick do YOU think you are? Is that a special or lucky ball? How important is the score? Do you have big bucks riding on the round? Are you on suicide watch? Your call!

Wet fairways: I hate them. Doesn't matter whether it is rain or dew induced, my brain goes into lock down when I'm required to hit off a wet surface. I hit it too fat or that worm burner stops cold. Overcome your phobia. Something I have yet to do. Foot wedges won't help you here.

The Ground: This can interfere with almost every potential shot you can possibly have to make! Too much grass, too little grass, sandy surface, rocky surface, up hill lies, down hill lies, side slopes, wet turf, muddy turf, aerated greens, I can go on and on. That stupid ground has ruined too many potentially good rounds. Why can't it all be the same? Courses should go to Astroturf. I bet I could worm burn a par four green from the tee box, providing no water or traps were in my line of fire.

A whomper should receive hazardous pay for hazardous play. Rounds of golf can be expensive. Try to get your money's worth by hitting the ball a lot, taking do-overs and by strategically utilizing foot wedges. Don't do this at the expense of your partners though. Look at the expressions on their faces. You'll know if you are making the right or wrong call. Be warned. Wagering on play changes everything. That's why I never bet on my game against anyone else's. I'd have a better chance winning a lottery than winning a bet on the links.

Hitting My Woods

There is a variety of fairway woods and any caliber of golfer can and will use them in the typical round. At the tender age of twenty or so, picking up the pasture sticks for the first time, I had this natural ability to hit fairway woods. Call it a gift. Ball sitting pretty, perched on a clump of turf, two hundred yards from the green; fairway woods, guaranteed. I wowed my fellow golfing buddies with my uncanny consistency to play inconsistently. Often, they froze in their cleats, mesmerized by how I could possibly do what I did so effortlessly. Now don't get me wrong, all of them used fairway woods. They just weren't as proficient as little ole me. Hitting woods off the tee box are not uncommon in our foursome. The key is to keep your eye on the ball which can be tough when you're supposed to keep your head down.

What always amazes me is that distinctive sound, somewhat amplified when hitting any fairway woods. It's an attention getter for sure; like the shot heard around the world. While whomping my way through an afternoon round I always try to visualize my next shot to determine if it might offer up an opportunity for me to hit fairway woods. Whether the woods are on the left or right side of the fairway, I seem to be able to deliver that perfect hook or slice to reach them. I bet tree huggers hate me as I chip away at their dreams.

I probably inflict more damage on loblolly pines than the dreaded southern pine beetle. One of my finer moments must be the result of a three-wood shot. I ricocheted off three trees in one shot. First my slice banged off a mature red oak a hundred fifty yards off the tee box and eighty yards to the right of my fairway. Then it glanced off a small sweetgum before hitting solidly off the pine spraying enough bark to start a mulch business. The pine sent my ball rolling back into the fairway one hundred and thirty yards from the white tees. Each contact with a tree emits its own unique sound. I have often been tempted to yell timber instead of fore. It seems more appropriate, don't you think? Those searching for Bigfoot might confuse the sounds with tree knocking.

Fairway woods may come into play for me anywhere and with any club. I am very versatile and can send one into the forest even with a wedge from the middle of the fairway fifty yards from the green. The woods could be seventy yards to my extreme right, but I am a professional whomper, so even the impossible is possible. That next shot from the woods to the green can be the miracle shot of the day or may slam that one tree in, or maybe not in my line. Full body contact looms large for those nearby, taking for granted the ugly consequences of my wood play.

If no fairway woods are in sight, you can count on me whacking that one tree out in the fairway that shouldn't even come into play. Driving range attendants cringe when I arrive with my large bucket of balls. They know that the motorized ball picker upper will serve no purpose in retrieving mine. Left then right, peppering the stand of pines marking the boundaries of the driving range. I think I've caused my neighboring whackers on the practice tee to flinch a few times hitting shots off the club toe. I hate driving ranges anyway as much as those tree huggers hate me but then again, that's another story in the life of the Original Whomper.

Sometimes trees can be your friends on the course. We've all launched those drives deep into the wood lined fairways figuring we'd have to hit a mulligan or take the distance and a penalty stroke. Behold, the ball bounces back into the fairway tossed by a friendly tree or possibly a befuddled woodland creature. We too often give those trees the credit assuming a squirrel hadn't been responsible for the event.

Fairway woods contribute to most of our golf rounds. We have a little thing called the root rule. If you don't like where your ball landed, do your best to locate a tree root nearby that will interfere with your next shot. We don't want to damage our club. Take relief. Move your ball and fluff it up. Strategy can come into play if you take the tree out of play by moving your ball left or right. Just claim more roots until you find that perfect spot.

Yep, I'm a firm believer in hitting fairway woods. It's just part of my game and always will be. I just hit some better than I do others. I probably should have been a logger or maybe I have been in another life. See you along the fairway where the wildlife knows me by name.

Strategy is So Overrated

Let me state for the record that I totally understand the concept. Golf is a game of strategy. It's just not in my game plan. I don't do strategy or at least I don't do strategy well. Calculating yardage, verifying the pin placement, selecting the appropriate club or using the best brand ball for your play is serious business to most golfers. Guess I don't fit into that "most" category and don't take the game that seriously.

My assessment, strategy contributes to a stressful round as does having higher expectations than what you know to be reasonable. I know my limitations, plus I'm too laid back to let any game ruin my day or life. Those who play with me typically have a full appreciation of what they've signed up for within the first two or three holes. My game can be anywhere and everywhere. Anyone can strike the ball and send it long and straight. What's the point? Perfection leaves no challenges. A fairway is an overrated concept and lends to boring golf.

Seriously strategic golfers should never invite me into their foursome. That's why I don't perform well in those captain's choice, best ball type tournaments. I have no best ball and I certainly wouldn't be a captain's choice for a partner. Too much strategy for me. I receive a best ball invite because I'm usually a better than average putter. Heck I'll putt from thirty yards off the green when possible, Texas wedging it to the hole. Foot wedging a putt is not allowed unfortunately and that plays heavily into my game's effectiveness.

I find it amusing when my playing partners agonize over their club selections, determining if this shot requires their one-hundred-yard club or their one hundred twenty-yard club. I don't have clubs for ten or twenty yard increments. Here's my typical setup. I'm facing a hundred thirty-yard shot. Do I use my seven-wood or one of my numerous pitching wedges? I have nothing in between. I'm traditionally untraditional when it comes to the game of golf. Aiming is an over exaggerated art. My alignment is as unorthodox as it comes. My playing partners have stopped asking me if I know where I am aiming.

Most rounds I play old man golf using about four different clubs from my bag, more if you count my assortment of wedges. Par fours and fives; driver off the tee, seven wood or number five hybrid from the fairway, then a regular wedge one hundred thirty yards to ninety yards, 52° wedge between ninety yards and sixty yards, then 60° wedge for all others unless I'm using the putter, aka Texas wedge. Par threes, choices are wedge, a nine wood or my five hybrid, unless driver is required. Describing my game plan already sounds too much like strategy, doesn't it?

Yardage, I check it only to determine if this is a wedge or wood shot. One of my buddies has one of those Sky Caddies glued to his hip so he can determine the exact distance to the pin. Knowing the distance doesn't play into my game as much as direction does. My aim and direction don't always agree either. Knowing how far to hit it and then hitting toward that yardage is what makes my game so challenging. A hundred fifty-yard second shot to the green might be a two hundred twenty-five-yard third shot for me from an adjacent fairway. My rounds can be quite exciting to the watchful beholder. Ball selection is also overrated. Use a white one or yellow if you prefer. Living for a few years parallel to the green on Blackmoor's one hundred seventy-yard Par three, I became accustomed to collecting balls. I didn't have to buy balls while we lived there. I just waited for them to fall from the sky then sort and egg crate them for later use. I accumulated over three hundred with only one broken window. I would dump a dozen in the bag when I got low. My buddies often ask when helping me look for my ball, "what were you hitting? How'd you have it marked?" My response, "I'm not sure about the brand but it would have had somebody else's initials on it." I don't lose as many balls now because whatever we find must be mine, my claim anyway.

Reading the breaks on a green, bet that Sky Caddie doesn't do that for you. I've tried to be a little more patient and sometimes even squat down behind the ball to look for a slope or something. For somebody who doesn't stalk the hole from every angle for five minutes, I putt better than average. My toughest vice is waiting my turn as I'm a quick draw both on the green and in the fairway. Slow play is the kiss of death for my game. If I must wait, the mind wanders all over the place. If I did do strategy, then I could probably occupy those long intervals.

It's fun to watch someone plan their shot. "Should I draw the ball? Is this the place to use a fade? Hook it or slice it? Flop it or bump and run? Sometimes I picture a third base coach out in the fairway giving them the signs for the next play. I'd be taking off the bunt sign and having them swing for the fences.

Here's my game in a nutshell. I grab one of the clubs that I mentioned earlier to match the scenario. I hit it. It goes somewhere. If it's my tee shot, I'm ecstatic if it travels far. It doesn't have to go straight. If luck be with me, I address the ball and hit it again, and it goes somewhere else. If I'm lucky that somewhere else is toward the general direction of the green. If not, I'll whomp it again from where it landed. I keep whomping it until I finish the hole or reach double par. Double par is an easy score to keep up with on the scorecard. It just means I'm doubling my money's worth.

At the end of a hole I mark down my tally. At the end of the round I tally up the damages. If I'm around 100 or just below, I'm happy. If I ended the round with the same two balls, I originally pocketed then I'm bragging about the round. If I finish with more balls than I started, I had a remarkable round, and probably had an opportunity to do some nature trails. So goes my strategic approach to the gentleman's game.

Greenhorns

Embrace bringing a new whomper into your inner circle. If he's a true greenhorn and you play badly but he plays worse, you'll have someone in the foursome you can possibly beat. If he turns out to be better than you, then you'll have to scheme how to discredit and oust him. First try taking the newbie under your wing and show him proper golf etiquette, the group's playing philosophy and terminology. Being thick skinned is a requirement, not an option. Explain that bad play will be rewarded by relentless trash talking.

Remember, the greenhorn can be inflicted with cart confusion. To ensure they go to the correct cart, now is the time for you to use one of those sarcastic remarks while pointing to their bag and playing partner behind the wheel. Sometimes they will follow you from the green to your cart. A riding buddy doesn't always pay attention to where the driver parks the cart. Heck, sometimes they forget where they parked the cart when designated to do so. Adult beverages can play heavily into judgment and perception. This isn't always restricted to the newbies. Be forewarned of the seeds you sow.

I have never forgotten an incident that occurred many years ago during a round with the Kemet whompers. On the first tee box, Mr. Greenhorn removed his stand-up bag from the cart and set the bag up on the tee box. Making his first club selection and then completing his shot, he replaced the bag on the cart. In the spirit of fast play, we informed him to leave the bag on the cart until the round had been completed, even though it would have been a hoot to see how long he maintained this routine.

You must remind them when to hit their shot, not to walk in the line of a putt, not to talk or back up the cart while someone else is striking the ball, and that they are responsible for keeping up with their own score. Oh yeah, they buy the first round from the beverage cart girl.

The newbie must be taught the rules. In no particular order, here they are.

Telling them to "pick it up" for a gimmie means they still count that as a stroke.

You must remind them that they can't keep making a shot until they make one that they like.

Explain you'll give them one mulligan per nine, not nine do-overs per hole. And, a do-over is actually a mulligan and there are not endless.

Bad shot. Advise them to hit a second, a provisional ball. Remind them that if they find their ball, to pick up the provisional. And then reinforce that they don't get an optional provisional on every hole. There is no endless provisional where the provisional is played every time instead of the bad shot found.

Make sure that you tell them to bring plenty of balls. And for them to always keep an extra ball in their pocket. It speeds up play.

Ask them if they have heard of a practice range. It doesn't matter if you lose those little stripped balls there. Or maybe tell them to keep a dozen range balls for play later. They can always say that yellow black stripped Wilson Staff balls is their chosen brand.

Keep reminding them that the ball marker is placed behind the ball, not in front of it on the putting surface. I once saw a playing partner place the marker in front of the ball and then when he replaced the ball, he placed the ball in front of, instead of behind it, inching towards the hole. Did he know better? Maybe. Maybe not.

Most greenhorns will ask for your assistance. Please try to be helpful.

Did anyone see where my ball landed? *Try looking on the tee.*

Did anyone see where my ball landed? *Give it a second. By the way, cover your head.*

Did anyone see where my ball landed? *You hooked it. See that huge red oak tree just to the left of the fairway about a hundred yards out. It should be about 150 yards further left of that tree. Here, wear these snake chaps. You have my cell phone number, right?*

What am I doing wrong? *You did nothing wrong. I'm the one that invited you to play with us.*

Can you see what I'm doing wrong? *It's too painful to watch.*

Can you help me straighten out this slice? *Drink more beer. Pass me one while you're at it. Try closing your eyes.*

What did I do wrong? *Actually, it was a very impressive drive. Those guys over in the other fairway liked it. They're still pointing and yelling that you are number one. Yelling 'fore' works much better before you almost hit somebody.*

Which club should I use for this shot? *Which club have you not tried?*

Feel free to give advice if they're shy about asking.

Using your wedge on the green is a poor club choice. You might want to try that putter in your bag. Yeah, that's the one.

You're only eight feet from the hole. Nice shot. You're only twenty feet past on your first putt, ten feet past on your second putt and only six feet past the hole on your third attempt. Your putting is improving. You should be close to the hole within the next couple of putt-bys. Have you tried one of those courses that have windmills and dinosaurs?

Too much back swing, that's why you can't hit the green with your putts. You have your putter confused with your driver as you seem to be able to hit it further. Try using your putter on the tee box next hole.

Where'd you learn to drive? You're a natural. I've never played with anyone that could operate a cart as well as you.

Don't go tin cup on us. If you hit a ball in the water, just go ahead and drop one on the other side. Six in the water is not helping anyone unless you're still using those yellow stripped Wilson Staff balls.

Take what clubs you need, walk on up and finish out the hole. We'll meet you on the next tee box or the one after. Tell that group behind you what you're doing when they catch up.

It's okay to hitch up with one of the groups that are behind you, even if you must screen several until you find one that can maintain your pace. And, have a nice round. Join us on the 19th. We'll celebrate you finishing your first round.

We've chipped in and bought you lessons. Call us when you graduate.

Nice shirt by the way, very colorful, it makes it easy for us to locate you in the woods.

Do you bowl? A 150 average is not bad on the lanes.

You're the newbie and are required to bring the beer until you score below 120.

When we say you hit it like a girl, we mean that in a good way. Most girls do hit the ball that far or even further.

Please pass me another beer before you tee off. No, beer will not necessarily help your game, but it does help mine right now.

Try cursing after you whiff and whomp the ball.

Throw your club only after you have struck the ball first.

I know your driver seems to be the correct club based on your previous driving but let's try your nine iron on this 110-yard Par 3.

Reward good shots.

That was a nice ten skipper across the pond. It almost made it that time. You get to drop it on the other side. Hope that was one of those stripped balls.

Great shot! Worm burned it off the tee, down the cart path, across the bridge and onto the edge of the green. The only thing missing for me was a windmill or maybe a volcano!

Nice nine, you stayed away from that dreaded double par for the last two holes. Build on it. You're improving.

Nice hole out for an eight, a natural snowman that time.

Finish the round on a positive note.

Really, you need to find a foursome of peers.

Your first round is a mere blur. Yeah, I know. This is your first round.

Was Happy Gilmore your favorite golf movie?

*You played just like Charles Barkley
(thinking…terrible…terrible…terrible)*

I'd hold off on buying new clubs just yet. Save your money for some well-deserved lessons. Remember, keeping score is not required on the driving range.

We're so glad you joined us. We'll keep you as our designated fourth when we have an opening. No, you don't have to check with us. We'll keep you posted.

No, I don't think we're playing next weekend or any weekends for awhile. But your game has really improved. You've almost got it below 140 now. I think you're ready to ask the boss out for a round.

Closest to the Pin

Anyone that has ever witnessed me playing golf fully understands my reluctance to wager on my performance. Unlike Pete Rose, I prefer not betting on myself or my team because I know my limitations. Unfortunately, when whomping the ball, friendly wagering can be anticipated as part of the game. I don't mind forfeiting my buck here and there for closest to the pin, longest drive or winner of a captain's choice, but I draw the line and refuse to do the big bucks betting.

Often during our Wednesday after work league play, we would all toss in a dollar for team lowest score. The winning foursome might clear five bucks a piece in a captain's choice format. Of course, we would toss in another dollar for closest to the pin on one of the par threes. Don't ask me to hold the money though. I really don't need this distraction and refuse to be the potholder. I don't do the money collecting or banking duties. It just makes it more painful when I must forfeit it over to someone else a second time.

Strategy and greed go hand in hand for many of my golfing buddies when that pot of gold is on the line. Sorry, I just can't get excited about my chances to win the big one; the big one being less than twenty bucks in most cases, before the four-way split. Everyone enjoys taking my money and how sad for them. Beating me is nothing to brag about. I suck tail pipe most of the time. It's a contribution, one that I can't deduct from income taxes, even though it could be considered a charitable event, from my pocket to yours.

I toss my buck in just to be social. Why should the plan be to always shoot for closest to the pin? Let's try something different like closest to the green or better still, closest to the tee box after everyone has teed off. I could win that one hands down.

How about these?

Closest to a fairway (must be your own) – bummer!

Most bunkers hit in a round (if you hit out of one into another then back into the previous trap a second time, you can count both)

Most skips across a water hazard (ball must reach dry land on the other side to be valid)

Most fairways hit (your fairway doesn't count)

Longest worm burner (must be in your fairway)

Highest number of putts on a single green

Highest number of lost balls (must at least attempt to find them)

Highest number of found balls (must subtract your lost ones from this total)

Most impressive hook or slice

Most impressive pop up off the tee box (loft and distance considered)

Club tossed the furthest without breaking the shaft (technique is important)

Most curse words by an individual in the round

Most number of trees hit in any single shot (hitting same tree more than once counts if you hit a different tree before hitting the same one again)

Best dressed

Worse Dressed (wearing racing or beer logo tee shirts and hats can be shoe-ins)

Most irritating cell phone ring to disrupt a round (must prompt someone to claim a do-over, or at least curse and give you the look)

The longest "Dukes of Hazard" cart jump (ejecting partners and/or coolers earn style points). Driver must remain in the cart to qualify.

Most adult beverages consumed (developing a slur or stagger warrants bonus points)

Another valuable lesson. Select your potholder wisely or you could get burned, no pun intended. The group allowed a young lady participant to hold the closet to the pin pot figuring she was the only female and best qualified to complete this task. When the round had finished, they asked her for the prize money. Well how do you reckon that went? *Not too good!* She had spent most of it on beer during the round. One must hydrate and besides, she didn't bring any cash and golf course beer is not cheap. Now what was she thinking? What were we thinking? Consumption of large quantities of adult beverages in the hot sun tends to make one very thirsty and can distort one's ability to rationalize. Guess she bet on herself to win and forgot she didn't hit the green. She didn't spend my winnings anyway, so I really didn't have a dog in the hunt.

I should just stick to bowling. Triple digit scores are good, and my bowling score is about the same as my golf score. A hook can be good thing but only if you can control it. I don't have to worry about how far I am from the green. No bunkers, just those fairway cutters on both sides. And there are no water hazards unless someone sweats on the approach. There's no score fudging as scoring is automated now in most establishments. You can yell all you want while your opponents make their shots. I'm better at closest to the pins and occasionally win the pot.

I Get No Respect

Rodney Dangerfield, may he rest in peace, was on to something with his routine about getting no respect. We 'whompers' have low self-esteem typically as a result of the crap we receive from our playing partners. All is fair when it comes to trash talking on the links. Learn to deal with it and dish it out or stick with FFF (forced family fun) on the putt-putt course. Missing the mouth of an alligator from the tee or hitting the blade on that spinning windmill can happen to anyone.

First time out, our bud, 'The Ragin Cajun' had this free-standing bag, one with legs that pop out, so bag doesn't tip over. On the #1 tee box at the Cedar Springs golf course in Greenwood, S.C., he unloads his bag from the golf cart and carries it to tee box, sets it there while he makes his club selection. Why yes, we did razz him. Probably should have kept our mouths shut to see how many times he removed it from the cart; every tee box, every shot, take it with him to the green? He sure was proud of that new bag. The clubs were of little help though.

Always wear those cleats. During a company tournament at the Persimmon Hill course in Saluda, S.C., a first-time player wears his nice penny loafers. Early morning dew still twinkling on the grass, he swings not once but three times on a slight slope behind a sand trap, disappearing and falling on his duff every time. Those off-white pants were green from belt line to the back of his knees. I had to turn away to conceal my laughter. He got even on the fourth swing as he banged the ball off the club toe and nailed me in the center of my back standing seventy yards parallel. I dropped to both knees and I now had grass stains marking the fall.

Asking at the Blackmoor pro shop in Murrels Inlet, S.C. if our other two playing partners had arrived. The attendant replied, "Yeah, he and his chunky little fat kid were at the driving range." John, about fifty and Pat, about forty, were not related. Hence, moving forward, we dubbed them, John and his chunky little fat kid when they were paired in our group. Same two, when both were wearing their

Clemson Tiger matching wear, were called *Clem* and his chunky little fat kid, *Son.*

Our Obsessive-Compulsive bud sweats pails of water on those hot summer days, especially on his backside. I once reminded him to wear his *Depends* next time. We ran with that one for a while. OC didn't find it quite as humorous as we did which caused us to turn it up a notch. Now he wears those stay cool and dry clothes. He still sweats profusely though.

One of my former whomping buddies, blind in one eye, had a bit of a depth perception problem when trying to strike the ball. A one-eyed-windmill-wonder, he'd whiff the ball so many times in a row that I'm not sure he paused between shots. Such profanity I've never heard from anyone. He's the bag totter from an early story. Originally from New Orleans, the *Ragin-Cajun* did let it fly after every miss and missed he did way too often. Last I heard he was back home living off crawfish, pinching the heads and sucking the tails.

Those five-foot putts that come up two feet too short prompt a, "you hit like a girl" raze. On the other hand, those five-foot putts that end up twelve feet past the hole, prompt, "back, back, back…out of the park, *Hank Aaron!*"

And one final note, when your shot banks loudly off a house, condo or automobile and you venture to retrieve it, always look back at your partner sitting in the cart as you pick up the ball, especially if you have homeowners glaring in your direction, "Hey, I found your ball, Carl. You were hitting that Intec, right? Looks like your initials."

Nature's Wondrous Waterways

Lakes, ponds, creeks, canals, reservoirs, ocean, mud puddles and rain-soaked bunkers, those pesky water hazards have this magnetic pull on my golf balls, no matter what brand I decide to use. Heck spit or piss on the ground and my ball has the uncanny ability to seek out moisture content. Besides, one doesn't purchase golf balls; each box comes with a rental program and limited warranty. There are no floaters. The balls are weighted carefully by the various manufacturers; thus, buoyancy is not guaranteed, a conspiracy that can't be denied. This is job security, building a business on repeat customers.

Sure, each will lay claim to the fact that their balls will go the furthest but going far doesn't always equate to clearing water. I know what you're thinking, that's my fault. Hey, I use clubs that proclaim to hit true, straight and long, very forgiving. To Quote *Jeff Goldblum's* character, Dr. Ian Malcolm, from *Jurassic Park, The Lost World*, 'Nature will find a way.' That's me, a natural force to be reckoned with, slicing and hooking the perfect forgiving club with very little effort. Perhaps they should allow someone like me to test drive these clubs before professing to such ludicrous gibberish. I don't believe these robotic mechanisms take into consideration the whomper or hacker factor, the uncanny ability to pull off the unthinkable.

Overcoming the subliminal overtures offered by a pending water hazard is no easy task. In between the ears lies the problem. It's not a good omen when I spot cooters, frogs and flopping fish on the green as I prepare to address my approach shot. Perhaps animal instincts are spot on when I'm attempting to clear the water ahead. Repeat after me, 'I see nothing but fairway. I see nothing but fairway ahead.' Worm burners normally work on any fairway, but this is a bad technique if that fuzzy oasis is strategically located between you and the green. Topping the ball may not be the best strategy either. That imaginary plush green landing strip you have visualized comes with consequences and sound effects. Can you say splish splash? If you're lucky, you will have a drop area on the other side to debunk the urge and requirement to hit another. Going Tin Cup can be costly, mentally and emotionally. What's the real value in seeing just how many balls you can sink? It's not like skipping rocks. Wet is wet and rocks are in abundant supply. How many times do you need to witness it going deep to get the point, right? Plus, it only slows downplay and you wouldn't want to face the wrath of the ranger or be shunned as the member of your foursome holding up the round. If you've seen one splash, you've them all.

Whomper Strategy: Use an old ball or one of those with the little black stripes around it when setting up your water shot. I call them the Range brand, easily picked up on any course. Come to think of it, maybe I should make this my preferred ball. There are a lot of them in those buckets you purchase at the driving range. Red Stripe is a beer so why can't Black Stripe be the hottest new brand on the market? Some courses like Arrowhead offer the range and practice balls for free. Park your bag and fill it up is all I'm saying. Toss pride and honesty out the window, which are predominant traits of the golfer anyway. Most have no pride and cheating comes into play as part of the round's routine. You're only a cheater if you're caught red-handed or red faced or have no shame in flaunting your skill. Another advantage, when you hit your ball near a driving range, you can virtually claim any ball as your shot. There really is no shame in golf, especially if you dub this strategy, and strategy is in the eye of the beholder. It should be of no consequences to your playing partners what brand you choose to play. Consider oneself the trend setter of the links. Or just covertly slip a ball from your riding buddy's bag. His loss is your gain.

So, here's my point, leading into a recent round at the Heritage Club in Pawley's Island, a postcard course, fairways lined with ancient live oaks, bordering old rice fields and marshlands. Wetlands equate to watery challenges and not just in the fairways. Much of it bordering the right or left sides can be magnetically enchanting yet challenging to ball striking insecurities. I shouldn't really complain. My golfing buds and I latched onto a summer special offered up at Legends Resort one year. For the upfront fee of $139, our golfing privileges were paid in full commencing June 17th through September 22nd. After 2 PM, any day, including weekends and holiday, we can play the Legends three courses near Conway, Heritage Plantation in Pawleys Island and Oyster Bay in Sunset Beach for no additional charges for the entire summer, cart and green fees paid in full. Basically, after about four and half rounds of golf, we're playing free for the summer, providing we only play these courses. We intend to do just that. This was just too good to pass up. What were they thinking offering this up to us locals?

Back to this round with two of my fellow summer investors; a glorious rain free July Sunday afternoon at Heritage awaited our arrival for our 2:30 tee time. Just two days after the Fourth of July, we had the course virtually to ourselves. But, not to fret, even after the 4th, if I'm on the course, fireworks are guaranteed to be part of the round. I have an arsenal of explosive situations, never a dull round, and the unthinkable is always obtainable. The round began uneventful, if you discount me hitting the ball long and straight, an anomaly. I went bogey, bogey, par, par the first four holes, wowing my pals, prompting them to wonder if the mother ship had beamed down a clone. For the first eight holes I played extremely well. Number nine took some of the wind out of my sail after I landed my ball into a greenside bunker. There I stayed, me without my sand bucket, umbrella and folding beach chair. All in all, I was quite happy with my first nine score.

For every front nine, there is a back nine. Jekyll meet Hyde. How does one go from straight and long to boomerang slice by just circling the club house and pausing only long enough to reach the number ten tee box? Can memory loss kick in that quickly? In this case, bad golf was contagious. We went from shinning to sucking just that quickly. Granted, more water hazard opportunities laid in wait on the back nine, but liquid quicksand can't be blamed for poor ball striking too. I battled my way through a couple of double bogeys until #12's par four. Water crossed in front of the tee box and butted up against the full length of the right side of the fairway. I boomed a tee shot, a slight left to right slicing fade mere inches from the wrong side of the bank. I had exhausted my only mulligan much earlier in the round so I teed up my third shot after taking the penalty. Mirror image second shot found the shallows. I teed up my third, now striking my fifth and final shot. I nailed the shot, but it drifted even further toward gator infested waters. I'd settle for double par and watch my playing partners complete the hole.

For the heck of it, I dropped a ball at the one sixty mark and sent a full seven wood to the green, across the green and into the water behind the green; four shots, all wet. My playing partners finished with triple bogeys, one shot better than me. The next hole, a Par 3, of course, across the water, I hit a towering wedge, clearing the water only to roll off the back side of the green and disappear into a murky grave. On the next hole, I sent a third shot, worm burner into the water. All these watery woes were just practice for my ultimate accomplishment yet to come. Most anything that can be done badly on a golf course; I have either done or have witnessed it via one of my buds. How does the saying go; 'just when you think you've seen it all?' Well buckle up, this only gets better or worse, depending on your perspective.

Par four, extreme dogleg to the right, so I open the face of my club slightly, now thinking I'm Bubba Watson, capable of making the ball do what I want it to do. I'm not sure when I thought I was an actual golfer because strategy is not my strong suit. The ball came off the tee slicing right, way right, way too far right, heading into the trees and the houses that lined the fairway. I held my breath waiting for the familiar sound, my ball striking vinyl siding or a roof top. I heard neither, not even a solid tree knock. Feeling none too confident that I would find my Wilson, I reluctantly drove in the direction as last seen. My two pals trailed me in their cart, to help if need be in the Easter egg hunt. I heard voices as I approached, fearful that I may have rendered a child unconscious.

I rode slowly along the edge of the rough underneath the old live oaks and saw nothing that resembled Wilson. A voice from the adjoining yard said, "It's over here." I spotted four people at a bar height table all sipping on what I perceived to be adult beverages. None of them were offering to toss me my wayward ball so I feared this was about to become an ugly confrontation, especially if one of them was injured. A lady spoke up and said, "It's in the pool." I asked had any of them been hit and she said no. She repeated my ball was at the bottom of the pool. I told them they could keep it, telling them this was a first. I'd never bagged a pool before. I wasn't sure how to score it. One of the guys laughed saying take a drop, no penalty. I informed them that I had moved from living on a golf course because of people like me playing golf. They hooted, having a wonderful sense of humor.

I marked another notch on my driver shaft; condos, houses, automobiles, golf carts, tee markers, people, and now backyard swimming pool, completing my bucket list I'm thinking. Hindsight, I should have delivered my infamous line to those stating the ball was in the pool; 'Hey Eric, I found your ball. It's in their pool.' I'm just thankful no one was toes up in the pool. One thing for sure, it couldn't have been premeditated or intentional because I never know where my balls are going until after I've hit them. I slice, hook, fade, draw, worm burn, pop-up or shank at any given time. I'm just as surprised as anyone with the outcome and I am notorious for being consistently inconsistent, an unorthodox grip and swing guaranteeing anything is possible if you set your standards low enough. Why even attempt to improve on imperfection and become just another predictable and boring accomplished golfer. Not just anyone can lay claim to wetting their Wilson in a pool.

My watery ways were not over just yet. We approached number eighteen, a long sweeping dogleg left then right, with water in front of the tee box. The watery trap was also bordered by a lake on the right the entire distance, looping back in front and behind the green. Nestled on the bank just ten yards in front of the tee box was a four-foot gator. Across the water lay a second one and just over a hundred yards away, rested four more gators ranging six to over ten feet long. It gives greater meaning to water hazard, the gators' private swimming hole. I cranked a long drive down the center, well away from the dinosaurs sunbathing along the lake's edges. I topped a seven wood, rolling it less than a hundred yards, still leaving me too long a shot to make the green. I laid up perfectly, my third shot giving me a simple chip over the water and to the green. I took out my trusty sixty-degree wedge and worm burned my fourth shot into the water. Here we go again, out in four, hitting five. Number five, low and zipping, bounced along the water surface before striking the wall on the other side. Out in six and whacking number seven and now very short on patience, launched a high and long wedge, right of the green and deep, deep in the water. I conceded a double par ten, ending a horrendous back nine. I must have lost over a dozen balls, most on the last nine holes of play. Summer special. Free golf. Build on that thought and forget the hazards of watery play.

The Flim-Flam Man

Have you ever seen that classic 1967 movie, *The Flim-Flam Man* staring *George C. Scott* as *Mordecai C. Jones*, a drifting con artist who makes his living playing tricks on people in the South? Well, I think my next-door neighbor may be *Mordecai* reincarnated. If not, he certainly missed the casting call for his shot at this role.

We lived on Murrells Inlets' Blackmoor golf course for about five years, actually adjacent to the green and fairway of a one hundred seventy-yard par three. Now when my wife and I were relocating from Abbeville, S.C., I never envisioned us residing on a golf course. I play golf and whomp the ball terribly. Why in the world would I choose to live on a course with people like me out there playing? Our realtor scheduled twenty-seven homes for our viewing and luck would have it, most were on a course. Welcome to Myrtle Beach, a golfer's paradise.

Now old *Mordecai,* a seasoned veteran as was *George C.*, is a golfer too, much better than me. Living on this hole, we both receive an ample supply of free balls from errant tee shots. I think I've accumulated over 300 balls, one broken window and a section of cracked siding in the first three years we lived there. *Mordecai* too has received siding damage. Neither I nor he have replaced the strip of vinyl siding. This is where we differ, and I separate myself from Mister Flim-Flam. The plot thickens.

Mordecai, retired and loving it, often relaxed on his back patio watching the unsuspecting prey as they attempt to will the little white projectile from tee to green. Unfortunately, many do not complete the journey and end up in our yards, banging off our roofs or slamming the siding with a very distinctive sound. This is the price one pays for living on a golf course with my clones roaming the fairways. By the way, I've never hit into mine or *Mordecai's* yard so far when playing this hole.

Mordecai bless his heart (that's a phrase we southerners use), had set the trap, and just like a spider, waited for someone to stumble into his web. If and when a wayward ball struck his house, he sprang into action, retrieving the ball before the victim arrived at the scene of the crime. Unless totally embarrassed by the wayward shot, the golfer will usually take a quick look for that ball.

With ball clutched firmly in hand, *Mordecai* motioned his newfound friend over to assist him in locating his tee shot. The trap had been set. He asked, "Did you just hit this ProV?" And of course, he nodded yes and apologized for hitting the house explaining the shot just got away from him. "Let me show you what your little ProV did." *Mordecai* then ushers his mark over and points out the cracked siding. Now let's clarify Mr. Webster's definition for flim-flam – to swindle; cheat. The trap has now been sprung.

Mordecai has now convinced Mr. ProV that he inflicted this damage to the siding. Not to worry he tells his victim, "I have extra pieces of siding in the garage and guess I'll have to either replace it or have someone replace it for me." Poor Mr. Pro V asks, "How much would it cost to install?" In the web now, there is no escape. He replies "I'm not sure. I've never installed siding." And the golfer now wishing to return to his foursome says, "Here's a twenty, will that help?" The deal is closed. The ball is handed over to the poor sap. *Mordecai* returns to his web, sips on a cocktail and waits patiently for the next victim.

He shared the story of his windfall with me once again. I asked him if he had replaced the siding and of course he had no intentions of doing so. Embarrassing but the life of a flim-flam man is not about integrity. Just watch the movie when you have an opportunity. To complicate the lives of our wandering ball searchers, *Mordecai* strings fishing line along the yard perimeter facing the course. They walk into this line and most of the time it stops them cold from entering his yard and trampling the flowers and shrubbery. I say most of the time, because it still requires some integrity not to encroach and trespass, lacking in many weekend visitors to the Grand Strand.

Mordeca will call down the golfer who fails to yield his warnings. He'll verbally confront the golfer that attempts to strike a ball from either of our properties, something they should know better about doing. I hail him for being proactive. All said, *Mordecai* is not without heart. He leaves a couple of buckets of ball on the back edge of his property line encouraging those that hit balls in the yard to leave them where they landed and simply replace it with one from his offerings. I'm sure there are no Pro V's in that bucket. Of course, the exception, hitting the house, changes the rules of engagement and he again turns flim-flam.

I should rent that old classic and invite the neighbor over to watch it with me. It would be interesting to hear his take on *Mordecai C. Jones*. Something tells me that it would make no impact. I wonder how much money he's collected off my damaged siding, pulling the same scam while I work my daily 7 to 4 job. Supplemental funding for a fixed income I suppose. Hit them straight on number two or he may flim-flam you too.

Raspberries and Rulings

Golfers like to trash talk or just plain razz their fellow golfing buddies. Rules are only good when the rule helps your score, not your opponents. Remember, the score doesn't really matter, especially if you're playing badly. When the game turns really ugly, find a happy place and quit keeping score. Declare a practice round and hope you don't birdie or hole one. If you do, begin rescoring once you make that first acceptable score.

The all-inclusive excuse for the bad shot, *I'm looking up*. A cruise ship golf pro explained that it is physically impossible to look-up in the middle of a shot and demonstrated why this was mere myth. I still think you can look up.

"You're going to like it," Carl shouts as my ball then rolls into the water or sand hazard or worse. Carl, please refrain from calling my shots good until the ball stops rolling. Your perception is badly skewed. Premonitions from your lips rarely end in great consequences for my golf shot. Let's face it; calling them like you see them is like a blind man telling me I'm standing to close to the ball.

"I've lost my wedge head cover." After a quick search with no cover to be found, "Oh well, I have others at home." Seems that Mr. Obsessive Compulsive keeps an extra set of head covers stashed away. Imagine that. Do I give him heck? Guaranteed...

The "you were talking while I was hitting" do-over. This one has been way too prevalent in our group. We all tend to imagine we heard those little voices somewhere that distracted us, prompting another free shot. "You were talking, do-over! I think you moved, do-over! You opened that beer, do-over!" Funny, no one ever calls a do-over when good shots are made, regardless of how much whooping and hollering is going on behind us.

There is no such thing as a dishonest or unfair foot wedge if you maintain eye contact with your partner while in process of adjusting the ball's position. They didn't see it, it's fair. Root rules always apply. Trust me, even grass has roots which can justify repositioning your ball. We're not professionals so why risk harm to life or club.

Use of chain saws are not permitted, however, you may twist or break that tree branch, or pen it firmly behind another before attempting your shot. Better still; ask one of your cart buddies to hold the tree limb out of your back swing. Remember to ask them not to release it until you have completed the shot and cleared the area.

Rock hard sand in the hazard: "I can't hit out of this crap," he yells. "Crap must be every where" is the proper response to this complaint from your buddy. Okay, so rake the sand thoroughly to fluff it up then replace your ball strategically on an elevated sandy tee. Complain about the wet sand if you still don't make it out on your first attempt.

Three attempts and the ball is still in the bunker, however, most of the sand has now been deposited on the green. The proper call, "Are you finished sandblasting with that wedge, now? If so, either pick-up or just place it on the grass." Counter that sarcastic remark by only counting one bad shot. The others were mere replays of the first.

Hit the ball in the water and there's no drop area on the other side, declare one. Pick a spot that improves your chances of greening the next shot. All is fair if there is no designated drop clearly marked.

While removing all pine needles, pinecones, sticks, pebbles and other debris from around your ball, it often requires that you strategically reposition your ball in the rough afterwards. Your playing partner remarks, "Do you need a leaf blower, or will a rake suffice? Why don't you place your ball on the green and call that your shot?"

"Let's plan to go fishing after the round. You've certainly uncovered enough bait with those trenches you've been digging."

"Were all those turtles on shore before you hit your three balls in the water? Apparently, there is safety in numbers."

If your ball skips ten or more times across the water, you receive a free drop on the other side even if your ball doesn't make it to dry land. Seems fair, doesn't it?

If one whiffs at the ball or digs a trench behind it without making ball contact, then a stroke can't possibly apply. Just declare, "I didn't hit it then try again. Let's face it. We're not PGA card holders so don't get caught up in the simple stuff."

It's proper to declare a double boggy for that double par if money is not riding on the outcome, however, you will be aided in tallying those strokes when wagers have been made. Keep in mind that gambling can ruin a friendly round. Funny, your partners will tell you to pick up a five-foot downhill putt, but you'll have to hole that one-footer if a buck is on the line.

One never requests assistance to find your ball when you know it is hopelessly lost. Bend down and declare you found it as you strategically replace it with a new ball. Try to at least use the same name brand. If you find your first ball afterwards and the shot was better, just declare that the first ball wasn't yours. It simply looked like yours. It's your word against theirs. They'll usually shrug it off unless money is involved.

It's acceptable to hit a fellow partners ball (1) if neither of you has the ball initialed and his is the better of the two, (2) he doesn't know what brand you're hitting, (3) you're in the trap and he's not, and you arrive there first, making the switch quickly, (4) You put his in your pocket and replace it with yours before partner arrives, (5) he's beating you shamelessly, (6) you don't like him or he's pissed you off, (7) if caught, you're able to declare you're intoxicated and thought you hit your own ball, (8) he's intoxicated and will not know the difference, (9) you're both intoxicated, (10) if it helps you brake a 100.

Remember, it's ok to trash talk and bend the rules among friends providing the friends can take the razzing and dish it back at you and you can take it. If you're playing with serious golfers, you're on your own. If you're bad as I, you have no business playing with real golfers. They really don't appreciate our natural ability. It is so sad to be so misunderstood. See you in the rough. Bring your foot wedge and an ample supply of do-overs.

Score Card Rules

All right, I concede that there should be rules on the golf course but what I don't understand is why they must reference U.S.G.A. Rules on the score cards. *U.S.G.A. rules shall govern all play. U.S.G.A. rules apply. U.S.G.A. rules govern play. U.S.G.A. rules govern play except where modified by local rules. U.S.G.A. rules govern all play unless amended by local rule.* Hey, we're Whompers. Most of us don't even know the meaning of the acronym. Heck most of us don't know the definition of acronym. And besides the touring professional, who really carries a U.S.G.A. Rule Book; certainly not the average guy?

As if we didn't have enough to deal with, each golf course tosses in its own little list of rules that may or may not comply with U.S.G.A. These typically include an assortment of out of bounds rules. We must contend with the meaning of the white stakes, yellow stakes, red stakes or that confusing water hazard flag that is not marking the hole on the green. Let's not forget the environmentally sensitive areas that will require referring to Rule 26/1 if you're unfortunate enough to whack your ball in the forbidden swamp land.

Oh yeah, the roads are out of bounds to the right of #1 and to the left of #18. I'm not even going to mention those shots that slam a condo, house or barbeque grill. Is it acceptable to retrieve your ball if no one is in the yard or comes outside after you rattle their siding? And don't play from their flower beds as you must take a drop and seek relief not nearer to hole. One of my playing buddies is notorious for relieving himself in the flowers whether his ball landed in the bed or not. He is specifically attracted to azaleas.

Rake bunkers, repair ball marks, and fill divots with sand provided on your cart. Look, there's enough sand on the golf course without us having to haul it around on the cart. I'm proud of those divots, especially the ones that could sub for a hair rug. Red wigglers need to surface for air sometimes. I'm just assisting them. What is a golf course without divots? It's part of the game, right?

Each operator of golf cart must be at least 16 years of age. Trust me, age shouldn't be considered as a requirement. We have members in our group that are triple that age and we won't let them drive the cart, but then again, that too is another story.

Please keep pace of play in mind. We always keep this in mind especially when the group ahead is going too slow. The most bazaar rule appeared on a score card in the Dominican Republic: *We believe a round of golf should take no longer than 4:20. Do not waste time. Be ready to make a shot when it is your turn to play and don't be afraid to shoot out of turn if doing so will contribute importantly to the progress of your group. All players are expected to keep up with the group in front. Golf ranger has full authority on the golf course to maintain rules and speed of play.* This was like *Gestapo* rules. Now doesn't that make you feel warm and fuzzy? I passed on printing my foursome's most colorful commentary for this advice.

Proper golf attire required. Now here's where we could probably use another rule book. I'll devote a segment on golf trending wear in a future chapter. Keep the rule simple; no jeans allowed, and collared shirt and shoes required. *Non-metal spike facility* appeared on one card. I didn't know they still made metal spikes. No tank tops and tee shirts. There should be exceptions for tourist visiting the beach. They do make sandals with embedded cleats. I have a friend that wears them. Flip flop friendly I suppose.

The most un-American rule: Coolers Not Allowed. Trust me, there are many counters to this rule, all of which I will cover in another segment also. The newer golf bags are wondrous inventions as are the creative minds of the Whomper. Beer totting golfers always have a work-around.

The listings of ball drop areas are a good thing even though many that we select are not always listed on the card. *For those rules not governed by the U.S.G.A. or local course you must consult your foursome* or just go out on a limb and make that call yourself.

We do have our own rules too. Rock and root rules, improving a lie, proper usage of a mulligan, when is a ball really out of bounds, rake use other than in bunkers and when to call a do-over are an intricate part of the round just to mention a few. Pencil these in if needed or just fluff them like we do. Fairways are fair plays; the jury of your peers will decide. Rules, sort of reminds me of that one about not removing that tag from a mattress. Who really knows or cares if you follow them or not unless you're in tournament play or it means something to your golfing buddies? When you shoot in triple digits, rules are the least of your problems. Just try to have fun, kicking and screaming allowed.

Scoring 95, Shooting 106

Integrity and honesty are what makes golf a gentleman's game. You either have it or you don't. Not having it doesn't prevent you from playing though. Some of the better whompers of the game have neither and score very well, exceptionally low as matter of fact. Plenty of things come into play to cause these elite individuals to derive their stroke scoring.

Denial, refusing to believe they just shot a double par. It's much easier to claim a double bogey or even an occasional triple than to mark down that dreaded snowman or ten spot. We're taught to keep up with our own score so who would know better? Some just suck at golf, but in a friendly yet competitive round, don't suck worse then claim victory over your playing partners with your creative scoring. Be assured, they will be tactful or maybe untactful in helping you reconcile your discretions by recapping every shot for you. Some will let it slide unless a wager is riding on the outcome but, be assured they are watchful and talking among themselves.

The need to break or achieve a target goal can prompt creative scoring techniques. Hey, we all make mistakes and your playing partners will overlook the occasional mathematical lapse. Chronic abusers wear out their welcome. Refusing to have a triple digit round ever can raise an eyebrow when your playing partners know you are capable of it. We all have bad rounds. Most can accept losing. After all, we're playing against the course, not the other partners. Don't boast about victories on the score card if the strokes are purposely skewed in your favor!

Inability to keep up with your strokes can be eliminated. Technology provides a means. There's an assortment of stroke counting devices available. The beads on a string are the simplest. Then there's the little handheld device where you click it each time you strike the ball. Go to any golf super store and you'll find an assortment of electronic gadgets. This alone doesn't solve the entire problem. You still must enter every stroke manually and there lies the problem. We're back to integrity, aren't we?

Too many adult beverages can contribute to the inability of the brain cells to connect the dots, especially if you're whiffing, whacking and whomping your way through the round. Ask for a designated score keeper if you're trying to strike your ball while still clutching the beverage. "Well John, what do you think I shot on this hole?" It depends on the rules of the day. You might have just shot a thirteen or scored a double par pick-up. Forget that bogey. It didn't happen.

Fudging a higher score than what was shot typically does not happen. For those trying to pad a handicap, they just intentionally blow an extra shot here and there. Integrity, should we mention that again? The problem, all golfers are not gentlemen. There's that occasional politician in the mix. And remember, just because some courses provide pencils with erasers, doesn't give you open season on that card.

Be wary of the partner that always wants to be the score keeper for the group. At the completion of each hole, if he asks what everyone shot but doesn't announce his shot count, that may be the sign of some card tweaking. The final tally is what counts, right? Who'll remember those skimmed strokes here and there? You'll be scratching your head, "Now how did he beat me with that 97 when I bettered or tied him on every hole? You then re-add the scores and tally the same results, not remembering what the partner shot on each individual hole.

Let's face it. Gentlemen really don't like to play the "you're cheating" card because you really like playing with the guy. Unless money is involved, it is best to just not let it get to you. Figure, if he can live with himself, why should I worry? Still galls you when you hear him recap the round and spurt out that score knowing it isn't valid. Then they ask you what you shot and, on the card, he beat you. It's then your choice if you decide to call him out.

I prefer to take the lead from my grandson, my cheap golf date. At eleven, he counted every stroke. Well, except for those penalty strokes after hitting one in the water or losing one in the woods. He hadn't quite grasped that concept of lose one, drop another ball then tally an extra stroke for replacing it in play. If he shot a seventeen, he wrote that seventeen on the score card and was proud of every single stroke. I eventually bought him one of those electronic scoring devices. It would not allow you to score higher than a nine. He would just carry over the extra strokes to the next hole and still manage to shoot that 150. Now that's integrity!

My Cheap Golf Date

The last chapter was the perfect lead in for this one. The grandkids are grown now, so this one is a blast from the past.

Playing the game of golf, one fantasizes about having that perfect partner. We pray for that special someone who can compliment our game and bring pure pleasure to a round on the links. A wife that loves to play the game can be an added bonus; especially if the two of you can leave the home and work grind behind to focus on the eighteen holes ahead. This is a rare find for most of us and is better left alone if your significant other doesn't share the same passion for the game.

We count on our favorite playing buds always being available for a round but often they can't obtain a golfing kitchen pass from that significant other. What does one do to prevent those unfortunate pairings with strangers? Sadly, there's no such thing as a rent-a-partner or is there? Nah, let's not go there. I offer a simple solution. Do you have a child that loves to whack the little white ball around and can maintain the pace required to not agitate those groups trailing you? Or better still, do you have a grandchild that lives close by that can be borrowed for the afternoon, no deposit required?

In my case, I have a ten-year-old grandson, Winn, who simply loves the game. He has his own clubs, balls, tees and a trend setting wardrobe. My grandson will play anytime I ask him. Heck, he would play every day if I'd take him. I must not give in to that temptation even for the love of a grandchild. Others just wouldn't quite buy into the concept. What makes taking my grandson such a sweet deal is that he plays free on many of the Grand Strand courses. Old grandpa doesn't take the wallet hit for bringing him along if I play my cards right. I've learned to shop around because many courses will allow juniors under the age of fifteen to play free or charge only the cart fee with a paying adult. I refer to my grandson as My Cheap Golf Date.

To ensure he maintains his cheap status, I always make sure we take our own bottled drinks and a plentiful assortment of snacks so there's no cause to hassle the beverage cart girl. Even with his cheeks stuffed with cheese puffs, his eyes light up as she approaches in her motorized chuck wagon. He treasures her strictly for her snack value. I try to distract him when I see her approaching because little blue eyes has this gift for pulling off the perfect con to access my wallet. Best laid plans foiled again as I fall under his spell.

I play after work on Wednesdays with my co-workers at the Quail Creek Golf Course and My Cheap Golf Date so happens to reside adjacent to the seventh fairway. Hawkeye spotted me passing through his neighborhood one afternoon on my way to the course. He followed me on his bicycle in hot pursuit to the clubhouse. Picture this. Here I am with my three golfing buddies unloading our clubs and changing shoes when he peddles up. For the record, he is not shy, not by a long stretch. He has this uncanny gift of gab capable of luring you into his web before you realize you're entangled.

As he shakes my partners' hands, he introduces himself as what else, My Cheap Golf Date. They howled and I had to do some quick explaining. He's a charmer and knows how to work the crowd for sure. He can milk a moment and quickly took center stage working his magic. In the day, he could have passed for a snake oil peddler. Those blue eyes can also transform him into the perfect little gigolo with the female persuasion but that's a story all by itself.

Being an avid Clemson Tiger fan, he eyed the orange tiger pawed character on one of my partner's golf bags. Working his southern charm, he soon had been rewarded with a Clemson Tiger club head cover from my partner. My unsuspecting playing buddy never saw it coming. He coughed it up to the little con artist, unable to control his actions. Needless to say, after that performance during his little cameo appearance, I invited My Cheap Golf Date to join me the following Wednesday because Quail Creek doesn't charge juniors to play their course. Besides, he attended a summer golf program there and knows all his victims, I mean the employees, by name.

His older brother, Duncan, had previously held the position as my original Cheap Golf Date until he accompanied me for a round of golf at The International Golf Club. The course did not charge for kids under fifteen with a paying adult. Paying adult would be me. That August afternoon the temperature topped the heat index at 113 degrees. We hunkered down and survived the eighteen holes, but I could never convince him to play with old grandpa after that hot round, temperature and not necessarily the scores. As I recall, he gave up the game after that memorable round and I don't believe he has ever picked up his clubs since. While he's no longer my Cheap Golf Date, I am proud of him just the same. He now plays with the Carolina Forest high school band and performs with their show choir.

My Very First Cheap Golf Date Duncan

He successfully threw his brother under the bus so he could sidestep any future invites from old granddad. He's happy, his little brother is happy, and I still have a Cheap Golf Date to carry on the tradition. His wisdom made all of us winners. I did ask their mom what I was going to do after the younger one reached fifteen. She laughed and told me I was on my own with that one. She added that there would not be a third grandchild in hers or my future.

A round of golf, $41.50; snacks from home, $5.50, purchased hotdog and a soda for old blue eyes, $8.50, My Cheap Golf Date, priceless and still cheap...

**Cheap Golf Date #2, Winn and Me Years Ago
At Possum Trot in North Myrtle Beach**

"Maybe I should give up golf and find a new hobby."

The Darndest Things

Whomping the ball with an eleven-year-old is like opening a golfer's Pandora's Box. You never know what wild and wooly experiences will be unleashed but you know you're in for an entertaining journey. Patience is the key. If you don't have it, taking your child or grandchild will only offer negative life experiences for junior.

My grandson, aka "My Cheap Golf Date", started playing with me around the age of eight or nine so he's a veteran at it now. He'd play every day if I'd take him. I'm going to have to cash in on those cheap date opportunities because once he turns fifteen, he then becomes a paying customer on the courses. For now, most courses allow him to play free so he's a bargain, a regular blue light special.

He accompanied me on one of my Wednesday outings for a peaceful afternoon on the links, not! Playing an executive course, my bud rolled his tee shot about thirty yards and still required another hundred to reach the green. He followed that up with another thirty yarder. My little bargain immediately pegged him a dirt dauber. Wonder where he learned that term? Little Mister Sunshine and I advanced to our balls near the green. Standing to the left of a trap, I warned him to watch out as Mr. John was about to hit his shot. Without batting an eye, he commented, "Can he hit it this far?"

The following are more words spoken by my little buddy and life experiences on the course.

He tells me, "I have to go to the restroom." My response: "We're on the next to last hole; two options, hold it or find a tree." He replies, "Which tree?"

He says, "I have a secret when it comes to driving the ball." My response: "What's the secret?" He replies, "It will cost you five dollars."

10-year-old: Never count strokes for balls that go in the water, woods, second tee-ups, or gimmies.

Grandson learns valuable lesson on the course. Balls will ricochet off trees and come back directly at your head. It's funny when they don't hit you.

Marking your ball: Doritos work every time. Who would have thought of using Doritos?

Values learned at an early age: "Where's the snack cart?"

Bartering for head covers: (ooh and ah over that Clemson club cover; guilt the owner in letting you have one.)

Too young to drive the cart, never too young to critique your designated driver: "Uncle Jerry, you're too jerky when you drive the cart."

I always encourage him to take plenty of snacks for the round so he won't bleed me dry from the cart girl. Uncle Jerry learns a valuable lesson. "Snacks are for me, not you. Uncle Jerry." Jerry remarks to me, "He kept pulling out so much stuff I thought he had packed a picnic basket."

Young Winn Singleton at Possum Trot Course

The 19th Hole of Horror

Relocating to South Carolina's Grand Strand in 2005, a Golf Mecca for many; my whomping frequency had no choice but to increase. I transformed from a twice a month player to twice a week. This had only marginal impact on the quality of my game. I remained a certified Whomper, or as my wife says, simply certifiable. One of our main reasons for making the four and half hour move from the middle of the Palmetto State to the east coast was to be closer to the grandkids. My new job helped pave the way.

Living here translated to more opportunities to participate in grandkid stuff like show choir performances, piano recitals, high school football, high school band performances, school plays and all sorts of fun stuff. It helped to have an eleven-year-old grandson (aka *My Cheap Golf Date*) who loved playing the gentleman's game. Most beach courses didn't charge for youths under the age of fifteen thus offering a two-for when I brought him along.

With Halloween approaching, the eleven-year-old had reached that age of too old to participate in trick or treating but not yet old enough to completely back away from the holiday. I could relate to that because Halloween remains one of my favorite holidays. I know, you ask what in the world does this have to do with golf. Stick with me. We're getting there. All kids travel down this path. I too made this transition from veteran trick or treater to 'I'm too old' to do this. The difference, I came up with an angle to reap the benefits of the holiday and still enjoy the masquerading. Simply said, I recruited a couple of my cousins and we constructed a Spook House. We then charged those that were traveling house to house a quarter for the price of admission or the equivalent in candy from the bounty they had collected. Remember a quarter was big money to us back in the day. We still got to wear costumes and have our candy too. Entrepreneurship, what a concept; we were entrepreneurs and didn't even know it.

I get it. You're still befuddled by my rambling ways. What does this have to do with golf? Hold on to your Trick or Treat bag, I'm getting there. This is called the set-up. Our little Spook House was a holiday success. We took in about twenty bucks in change and two grocery bags worth of their hard-earned candy. We cleaned house taking most of their collected booty. Kids couldn't get enough of our haunted house tour, returning over and over to pay for the fright night experience. A legend was born October 31st, 1966. My spook houses were recognized city wide. Build them and they will come. For the next couple of years, we built bigger and better ones until finally we outgrew the desire and moved onto to hot girls and fast cars, or was that hot cars and fast girls?

At the age of nearly thirty, I was recruited to build a haunted house for the Langley Milliken's grammar school Halloween jamboree. The school was in my childhood backyard, LA. Lower Abbeville, so why not. I had attended grades one through six there. I recruited a few friends and we worked our magic. We made more money that year with the staged spook house than the rest of the jamboree activities combined. My legacy continued, a legend if only in my mind.

Now let's fast forward and return to my grandson and his dilemma. His mom, aware of The Legend's reputation, asked if I would help him build a Spook House in their garage. He had decided to have a Halloween party and invite a few friends. Of course, I couldn't fight the urge, so I accepted. I don't do anything half-way and then they had so much neat stuff; life size and animated figures, realistic masks and props. Boy I wish they had had this stuff back in my day. We had to improvise and fabricate our own special effects back in the sixties. After accepting the task, I realized that Halloween would be falling on Wednesday. Oh no, not Wednesday! That was my golf after workday with my buddies. I couldn't miss an afternoon of golf just to recapture my past and make the grandson's wishes come true, could I? How could I possibly make this work?

Legend, it was time to strut your stuff. News flash, I decided to combine the best of both worlds. Golf meets Halloween! The theme for the Spook House would be simple, *The 19th Hole of Horror*. Conveniently their home was located on the 7th hole at the Quail Creek golf course, thus the theme did hold some merit. I immediately launched myself into a purchasing frenzy. Because it was so close to Halloween when we began our planning, I found that many stores had reduced their back to ghoul stuff considerably. Needless to say, grandpa bank rolled the project and I thoroughly enjoyed every buck spent.

We successfully decorated the garage with an assortment of special effects including a fog machine, eerie lights and scary sounds. I recruited assistance from both grandsons and one of their adult *kids at heart* neighbors. We were ready for the big show. I would be the official tour guide for the scary garage excursion. I only had to purchase a skull mask and skeleton gloves to round out my costume. I added these props to my black golf knickers and matching argyle socks, vest and black St. Andrews golf cap. I made the transformation to *The Bogey Man of the 19th Hole of Horrors.*

We decided to take no more than two victims, I mean kids, through our Spook House at a time. I greeted them at the entrance with an intro from my favorite childhood Friday night classic horror show, *Inferno*. With my best eerie voice, a *Bella Lugosi Count Dracula* knock off accent, I invited them through the haunted portal,

"Come in. I've been waiting for you. Venture with me into a world of strangeness; a world where reality slips past you like sand in an hourglass. Inferno! The meeting place of supernatural and the unknown." Prompt the crazed and deranged follow-up fiendish laugh

We were extremely successful in terrifying the partiers. The tour ended at the exit door with a putting contest for grab bag prizes with everyone a winner. Instead of a golf ball, our guests were putting golf ball sized eyeballs that illuminated on contact. I lived up to my reputation of Spook House Entrepreneur, fulfilling my grandson's wishes on my golf Wednesday. It doesn't get any better than that!

To my Whomper buddies as they try to survive a round, I say, *"It will only hurt for a moment, my friends, then, eternal life!"* Insert the crazed and deranged laugh once again. The Bogey Man has spoken.

The Bogey Man

Look Good, Feel Good, Play Good and Smell Good

One cannot play the game of golf if one doesn't look the part. I personally have always been a polo shirt and shorts guy, weather permitting. I keep it trendy, not tacky. A co-worker, six foot six or so, started wearing golf knickers. A walking billboard on the course, the golfing buddies thought the Ringling Brothers Barnum and Bailey Circus had come to town. Fred tried relentlessly to talk us into purchasing our own Par-4 Knickers ensembles and start a knickers chapter in town, but he had no takers. Most were too manly I suppose.

I, on the other hand, being fully secure with my masculinity, often wearing pink shirts or other pastel colors, pondered the possibility. I mentioned the golf knickers a couple of times to my wife, sort of trying to convince myself that I could really pull this off. I always liked Payne Stewart, but did that mean I could wear his wardrobe? With a birthday coming up she decided to purchase me a complete outfit. I must say, I was pleasantly surprised with the rather dapper black knickers, matching argyle socks, shirt, vest and the little flat hat.

Not until after my birthday did I realize the agony she had endured purchasing these as my present. Not convinced that I'd wear them, and they weren't cheap, she almost canceled the order several times. Residing at the time adjacent to Blackmoor's second hole green, a par three, we see all the golfers up close and personal as they play their rounds, sometimes in our back yard. About a week before my birthday I called her to the sunroom and pointed out how neat the two golfers looked wearing their matching knicker outfits. This quenched her fears and she stuck to her guns with my surprise.

People always ask me, "Where did you get that Payne Stewart get-up?" Simple, Golfknickers.com will fix you right up. I am the proud owner of four pairs now. I look good now but that doesn't always translate to playing well. One golfer, with a New Jersey accent, commented as I arrived for the round, "A player; must be a player!"

The then young grandson happened to see me dressed to the nine after a round and immediately knew he had to be a trend setter too. Tough to find miniature knickers so Mimi, aka grandmother, used concocted some pants. We purchased the rest (hat, vest, shirt, argyle socks) and parlayed this into his Christmas present. I ended up taking him to play golf the week before Christmas, so we gave him one outfit early. He paraded around like a child prodigy model and we had many photo opportunities posing on the runway, I mean fairway.

We're so adorable now, regular head turners as we whomp the ball down the fairway, making our fashion statement. Pulling up to a tee box, the grandkid hops out of the cart, crosses to the other side of an intersecting cart path and just stands there. I warned him of an approaching cart, and he responded, "I know, just showing them how good I look." Striking the runway pose is important on the course too. Oh, how we reap the benefits of our attire! The beverage girls are so taken by us. We're just so cute and huggable now. The chick magnet, old blue eyes; I mean grandson, draws them to us like bees to flowers, better than walking a cuddly pooch on the beach.

Sitting beside me in church, the magnet elbows me in the side. I give him one of those "what are you doing?" looks. Old blue eyes smiles and then pulls up his right pants' leg and shows me he's wearing his knee-high argyle socks. He's ready for the afternoon round. I just realize he's wearing his vest too. I immediately glance at his left hand to make sure he's not wearing his golf glove. He also sports that flat hat to school as often as Mom will allow.

Celebrating his eleventh birthday, his Mom decided to make it a golf themed extravaganza. The event, held at a local miniature golf course, Mom designs a golf ball shaped cake, and had a tablecloth resembling greens and all sorts of other golf related themes. Of course, Little Payne and Big Payne deck out in their golf attire. I sometimes refer to Little Payne as Royal Pain. We were party hits as we putted our way through the challenging course.

Playing the home course during Christmas week with a holiday twist, I wore Red, Green and White colors. The cart girl stopped to see if we required any additional Christmas cheer and smiled at me, "You look like a big old Santa elf; makes me want to just give you a big old hug." Well, I felt obligated to grant her Christmas wish and leaped from my sleigh and let her have her way. Heck, I'm no scrooge! For the first time, my playing partners regretted not owning knickers.

On another occasion, the beverage girl was struck by the little blue-eyed gigolo's outfit and comments, "You're just way too cute, sweetie." The magnet replied, "I can't help it." That's my boy. We're *Me* and *Mini Me*.

Our motto is *Look Good, Feel Good, Play Good.* He did embellish our little creed by adding *and Smell Good.* Now this stands as quoted. Dressed in our knickers *We Look Good, Feel Good, Play Good and Smell Good*!

Payne Stewart, we miss you.

Me and Mini Me at Wild Wing

The Coon Whisperer

When whomping along the Grand Strand it seems that I encounter more wildlife than what I am accustomed to in the upstate of South Carolina. These encounters happen much more frequently and can vary from comical, to annoying, to potentially deadly. There are some wondrous creatures along these marshes and waterways for sure.

On the upstate courses it's not unusual to see turkeys strutting their stuff, the occasional wandering deer and squirrels squiring hither and there. In the upstate we have grey squirrels and along the coast we have these mutated huge fox squirrels. Squirrels along the coast can never be trusted. They will forge from your cart shamelessly at every opportune moment.

Upstate or coast, warmer weather does increase your chances of snake encounters. These encounters catch both you and the snake by surprise, sending each in opposite directions. I'm okay providing I see them first.

Crows and the hunting birds of prey are mainstays along the upstate courses. The marsh lands along the coast have their egrets, cranes and heron. Canadian Geese and their droppings are prevalent every where. All these geese do is eat and crap up the course.

Fire ants are probably the fiercest foes we must worry with in the upstate, and they lurk on the beach links too. These little boogers will attack in masses when their mounds are disturbed and will cause you to peel out of your golf apparel and dance like you're trying to bring on a rainstorm. Mosquitoes can swarm in great numbers along the wetlands and will send you into that Macarena dance, slapping and covering ever inch of the exposed body.

Did I mention alligators? Too many courses have gators on the Grand Strand, especially inland. Heck, all we had to worry about in the upstate was a frantic chameleon falling into your draft beer.

Behemoths can be seen along the lakes or cruising the waters. Gator attacks rarely happen though, not that I'm going to tempt fate.

Okay. I think you have the picture now. Playing with three of my coastal buddies at the Wild Wing course, beach breezes blowing and humidity melting us like the witch in Oz, we plundered along making the best of another wonderful after work experience. Only a few holes into the round, something was up. Have you ever had that strange feeling that you're either being watched or worse, followed? We did. Suspicions confirmed. Soon we spotted a masked bandit flanking our every move from the rough along the edge of the fairway. Fortunately for me, I made this observation from the fairway instead of from the rough where I am accustomed to playing. We maintained a watchful eye on our adversary, knowing how sneaky those little critters could be. We could only imagine the havoc this larger version could wreak.

Becoming bolder, the raccoon cap wantabee left the cover of the brush and shadows advancing closer to our carts. Being the animal lover than I am, I tossed it a handful of pistachios and its boney little hands methodically made easy work of the shelled goodies, partaking of the bounty. Bad decision on my part; never feed the wild animals. As cute as they may seem, they are wild, not pets.

Leaving him in our wake, we completed the hole and advanced to the next tee box. My bad, our little friend had now tasted the rewards of good fortune. Knowing a short cut through the woods separating the fairways, he lurked a couple of hundred yards out, waiting for our tee shot. He didn't know who he was messing with though. I can't hit it 200 yards. The game, however, was on with the masked stranger.

As we approached our fairway shot, he advanced to check the cart's menu. I tossed him more pistachios to keep it busy while the four of us struck our shots. Making quick work, the little moocher again continued his hot pursuit. Short cuts, he obviously knew all of them. This time the masked bandit waited patiently as we arrived at the tee box, a 170-yard par 3 across the water hazard. Gerald, tiring of this little meddler, decided to send him packing. Frantically waving his nine iron, yelling obscenities, he charged the bandit and confused by the hospitality gone badly, the racoon scurried into the underbrush.

Gerald strutted proudly back toward the tee. Mission accomplished. He had conquered the wild beast showing the loathsome raccoon that man still ruled. Gerald with his back now to the forest, a bit of spontaneity kicked in and I figured this would be a great time for me to point behind him and yell, "COON!" This brainstorm far exceeded my wildest expectations. Gerald, certain that the coon had returned with vengeance, never glancing over his shoulder, tucked ass and began high stepping it toward the tee box. His arms were now flailing in some sort of defensive manner, club no longer the weapon it had once been. His evasive maneuver reminded me of a German soldier in a fast goose step. The remainder of the foursome joined in and pointed, confirming Gerald's belief that the raccoon now chomped at his heals. Made you feel like screaming, "Run, Forest, Run!" Alas, we were all belly aching with laughter, all except Gerald who had yet to turn and see how close the critter might be. Finally, he mustered the courage to locate the predator and of course, no creature was stirring, not even a mouse. He had been had by those masterminding the imaginary attack. We relived the moment for the remainder of the round, busting a gut along the way.

E-mails erupted the next workday as the Coon Whisperer chapter had been added to Whomper history. Gerald, now the newfound leader of the coon clan, drew notoriety where he would have least expected it. For many rounds thereafter, one of us would break into the coon dance, bringing the house down. The Whisperer would never be forgotten, even though we never saw our little masked buddy on the course again. I'm speculating that the little masked marauder was too embarrassed to be caught dead on the same fairway with Gerald. The Coon Whisperer had gained his place in Whomper history.

The State Bird

For the record, I am originally from the Palmetto State, born and raised, but we relocated to the Grand Strand about fourteen years ago. Previously we had lived in the South Carolina upstate. Resurrecting my love for the game, I soon discovered that the coastal courses pose unique obstacles and challenges that differ from those in the upstate. Any round of golf offers new twists such as the ever-present gators, many more venomous snakes, impressive fire ant mounds, the dreaded environmentally sensitive areas, brutal heat and humidity, unexpected coastal downpours and seasonally outrageous prices. Thank goodness for the local discounts.

Upstate courses have hills and millions of pine trees, no alligators, some snakes, fire ants, much cheaper golf options and fewer tourists, absent of the great northern migratory infiltration. Once the dust has settled, ultimately, *Whomping* is *Whomping*, wherever I hang my golfing cap. Swamp or wetlands tend to lurk at every dogleg or just off the tee boxes. If the course has no viable swamps then they just dig down a couple of feet and like magic, a water hazard grows from the once dry and barren land. These wetland wonders make for the perfect breeding ground for the South Carolina State Bird.

While winding my way through the fairways I often wondered why so many houses with pools had screen enclosers. I figured it must it prevent someone like me from nailing an unsuspecting sun worshiper or floater with one of my errant shots. It made perfectly good sense to me. Fact is they didn't fear golfers at all. Instead the screen shielded them from the state bird's persistent onslaught.

Lurking in the shadowed fairways, Count Dracula's offspring maintain a vigilant watch for those poor wandering souls searching for that bad shot. The first indication that you are under attack is when you hear that constant buzzing in your ears. It's when the buzzing stops that you hear the next sound that confirms you are in a perilous situation, *SLAP!* That sound is created by your hand now striking an exposed section of your body, reacting to the single fanged penetration of your unidentified attacker. Yes, the State Bird, a crafty blood thirsty predator, wreaks havoc on the locals and visiting tourists along the dark and dampened edges of the coastal fairways. Buzzing you at the most inopportune moments, it invokes those missed hits or stopped swings, prompting the call for a do-over.

Men on the golf course beware when heeding nature's call in Mother Nature's urinals. Remember that infamous 'Off' commercial. The gentleman in the commercial inserts his arm into a chamber swarming with the ravenous winged beasts, signaling dinner is now being served. Same test, subject now sprays his arm with "Off" repellent then inserts his arm again, the attackers now avoid contact. Picture this before stepping to the edge of the fairway and unzipping. **SLAP, ZIP and Retreat!**

My papa always said. "Son, do you know the best way to keep gnats out of your face? Cut a hole in the seat of your pants," Works with gnats maybe, but I wouldn't advise attempting this as a diversionary tactic for the state bird. If you're not with me yet, I'm referring to mosquitoes or skitters as some southerners call them.

When you find yourself being attacked, hit and run is your best option. One cart buddy remarked, "Hey, did you know these things can keep pace with the cart?" Try one of those torpedo dodging maneuvers used by naval carriers, just zig zag. If that fails, then it's time to make sacrifices if you're the one driving. Hard left and eject your partner. While they feed, rush to your next shot. Sometimes your bud must take one for the team.

If you're fortunate, like me, you have a natural deterrent. My wife has this uncanny ability to attract the state birds even if there's no indication of their presence. Feeling sorry for me one afternoon because I had no one to play a golf round with me, she gave in and partnered with me at Tupelo Bay, an executive course with lights on the back nine. I'd never played under the lights. Starting at 7 PM on a humid summer afternoon, a steady breeze blew the first nine making for a pleasant front nine. She walked most of the front nine enjoying the great outdoors while getting in a little exercise.

As darkness fell, the breeze disappeared, unleashing hordes of the waiting blood suckers. Having failed to equip the golf bag with 'Off' or 'Skin So Soft', they answered the ringing of the dinner bell and soon I heard that familiar **SLAPPING** sound. My wife attempted to fend off her relentless attackers. All they lacked was tenderizer. Final tally, after 18 holes she bested me with at least fifty bites. I had none. To be honest, I rarely ever receive a mosquito bite. That ended her golfing career and almost ended our marriage. She finds nothing humorous about me recanting this story. That next **Slapping** sound might be here smacking my head if I toss her another invite.

Nature's Wild Kingdom

While whomping the links, one has an opportunity to reflect and commune with nature, whether it is our choice or not. Mother Nature has this incredible knack for pushing her creations on us. What, might you ask, do we encounter? Let me be the first to enlighten you. The adventure begins here but I must warn you, the dangers lurk at every dogleg, each murky water hazard, on the darkest edges of the fairways and in those dreaded environmentally sensitive areas.

Squirrels, just innocent little creatures placed here to be whimsical and entertaining; however, a far sinister evil is camouflaged in those perky little eyes, twitchy bushy tails and animated spastic behavior. They are pure evil and are never to be trusted. They are the devil's pawns and do his bidding and do it quite efficiently. Now the cute little grey ones that scurry about the golf courses rarely ever pose any problems or threaten one's play, or do they? I have my own theory about these sneaky little messengers. I speculate they are scouts for the larger less timid fox squirrels. A fellow whomper, seeing these critters for the first time, grey or black fur with those white markings of the devil on their head, called them mutated elves. I tend to agree as the evidence supports his conjecture. These versions are sinister opportunist.

My playing buddy, leaving his cart unguarded, strolled toward his next shot with his trusty three wood. The elfin like creature, seizing the moment, hopped on board and immediately sniffed out his nutty nutritional nature bar. Returning to the cart after his shot, to his surprise, the mutation perched boldly on the seat behind the steering wheel, never flinching as he approached. Defiant, he stood his ground as it munched leisurely, grasping the bar in those boney human-like fingers. Completing a stare down, it finally exited the cart carrying the bounty. You could almost hear it whisper, *don't mess with a cult icon, golfer-boy.*

I almost became prey to one of these devilish creatures while making my putt. By the grace of a Ziploc zipped firmly, my pistachios were safe from its evil clutches. The mistake many of us make is tossing them a morsel as we pass them on the fairways. The hunter then becomes the hunted as they stalk our cart, waiting patiently for that next stop when we most certainly will leave the treasure unattended. Other encounters have proven my point. While on the first tee box at Myrtle Beach National, I left my sandwich tucked away on board my cart. The Ziploc didn't save it this time. Returning to the cart I caught a glimpse of my sandwich hopping across the opposite fairway, Ziploc firmly grasped in Mr. Fox Squirrel's mouth. I've since then lost an assortment of goodies to the bandits that call the golf course their home. One gentleman had his car keys taken up a tree by one of these culprits. I bet it pressed the panic alarm in hopes of locating the man's car.

I had to fend one off from my grandson as it approached him and gave no ground as he attempted to wave it away. My cheap golf date stomped his foot and waved his putter at the mutant raccoon. It held its ground and recoiled and then made a couple of charges. I was almost tempted to demonstrate to it how I can slice my driver, but instead I poked at it. It defiantly clutched the club head. It only retreated when it was ready to retreat and did it defiantly, not intimidated or amused by our attempts to discourage it. I don't know what makes these fury creatures so bold and aggressive. My Papa Bowie would not have tolerated such behavior. To him, a squirrel was a squirrel and squirrels belonged in a frying pan. "Good eating size," he would say.

Mutated Elf Owning the Tee Box

We played Whispering Pines June 1, 2019. I mention this round specifically because it had tragic consequences. While we were on the 8th hole we were under assault by a half dozen of these mutated menaces. They were swarming our golf carts and invading the tee box in search of handouts. To deter the invasion, I tossed them a handful of roasted nuts in the shell. This temporarily distracted them long enough for us to tee off and exit the area. See, I'm not such a bad guy. I often feed the wildlife during a round, the fox squirrels, cooters, coons and even the geese sometimes.

On the 10th hole as we exited the green we were greeted by another squirrelly beggar. We joked that his friends must have called ahead saying this group was easy pickings. I think it was attempting to unzip the pocket where the roasted nuts were stored. I ran him off, so I thought. And let me say that these little critters aren't easy to run off, too head strong and determined. I was the designated driver for our cart. As I pulled away, we experienced an obvious bump. I glanced back expecting to see something that had fallen from our golf bag. Instead I spotted the little marauder belly up and quivering. I had unknowingly murdered my first fox squirrel. Well, it was more like accidental homicide. I felt bad about what had happened, so much so that I remorsefully double parred the next hole. Sorry for the graphics but it happened. Why try prettying it up or pleading the fifth.

Let's move on. Canadian Geese, common on most southern courses, insult us with their droppings on the greens, misdirecting those potential birdie putts or in my case, boggy attempts. They can destroy a course, eating the grass and then pooping everywhere. Most will move out of your way if you approach them. One gent told me he nailed one off the tee box with his drive, dropped him dead right there in the fairway, unintentionally of course. Beware though, some can have a much darker side. A fellow golfing pal, Lowrie Parker, discovered while playing Hickory Knob State Park in McCormick, S.C. He had struck his approach shot across a pond and landed it in the water a foot shy of the other side. He then decided to retrieve his ball. The little goslings were scattered along the water's edge near the entry point. Mama and papa goose weren't too thrilled by Lowrie's close proximity to their little ones. The pair greeted him, wings flapping wildly, heads extended from their long goosey necks, beaks snapping and honking. Caught off guard by what he would later recall as a gaggle of geese, he did a funky all fours reverse crab walk, forgetting about the putter in his clutches. He had been goosed for sure.

Wild geese flock to all Grand Strand courses, eating the grass and pooping hazards.

Snakes. Enough said. We've encountered Satan's righthand demon too frequently at the water's edge or occupying the woods when we searched for our bad shots. This reinforces why one should stay out of the environmentally sensitive areas or what I call environmentally unfriendly areas, unless you're wearing snake chaps. Our errant golf ball becomes forbidden fruit. We curse and take a penalty stroke but live to play another day.

Then there are alligators. Just one simple rule; know that they are there. Many of our coastal courses are inhabited by these gigantic water lizards. Once as I retrieved my ball from a creek on an Edisto golf course, I had this eerie feeling of being watched. Glancing over my right shoulder as I plucked it from the water, less than five feet away, in a drainage pipe, lay a seven-foot gator watching my every move. My life became a blur. The first time I played Gary Player's Blackmoor course in Murrells Inlet, I hit my ball in the pampas grass and cattails along the #4 par three water's edge. Searching vigorously, I never did find it. My new neighbor on the # 2 hole asked me how I liked that ten-foot alligator at #4. '**Gator, #4; No One Told Me Anything About A Gator On #4**.' Things you need to know before doing what I did. Year and half later, the gator, a twelve-footer, had to be removed from #4 after the green's attendant witnessed it pulling a chocolate lab into the water for a quick meal. Where are Marlin Perkins and Stan when you need them?

The Rare Albino Mutation

Beware of Zombie Swans

Be Berry, Berry Quiet, We're Hunting Gators

People growing up in my era remember the iconic and classic Looney Tunes cartoons. Porky Pig, Foghorn Leghorn, the Road Runner and Wile E. Coyote, Pepé Le Pew, Tweety Bird and Sylvester, Yosemite Sam, Speedy Gonzales, Tasmanian Devil and Marvin the Martian were symbolic in the mostly Saturday morning antics. Of course, then there were the anchor characters of Bugs Bunny, Daffy Duck and Elmer Fudd. Today's world of being politically correct has ruined it for most of us. They've cried foul, too may of our treasured characters are cruel and abusive and often just too insensitive in their behavior. They're cartoon characters folks. They're not real. Watching them as I was growing up didn't transform me into a wife or child beater or a serial killer. I understood even as a child that they were funny and fun to watch. I got it. I still get it. The animated features that I view on today's television or at the theaters teach far worse lessons in my humble opinion. But I'm supposed to be sticking to whomping the golf ball tales, right? Just setting it up via my twisted narrative, getting there, I promise you.

I've mentioned the unique wildlife in previous chapters, especially the aquatic reptilian kind swimming and sunning at most courses. Growing up in the upstate of South Carolina we didn't have to contend with alligators in the water hazards. Heck, the water hazards themselves were enough to discourage most of us without adding man-eaters to the scenario. Well, I've not actually seen a gator eat a golfer along the Grand Strand, but attacks have happened in other areas where gators lurk. Now I have seen my fair share of humongous gators though. Elmer Fudd would say, "Be berry, berry quiet, we're hunting wabbits." Pointing his shotgun at Bugs Bunny, the waskely wabbit would rebut, "Duck season." To which Daffy would say, "Rabbit season." Eventually Bugs would win out resulting in Elmer firing his weapon at poor Daffy. "Despicable," would be his ducky response. Well, now it's gator season on the Looney Links. Here are some of my wildest memories of golfing gator encounters.

I've also already mentioned the twelve-footer that once resided on Blackmoor's #4 par three hole. After snacking on the Labrador, it was exterminated only to be replaced by a ten-footer that moved into the pond to take its place. I regret that I never took a photo of the behemoth that would make Troy on *Swamp People* shout, 'Choot-em!' I once joked with my cheap golf date when the monster occupied the tee box, to sit on him and I'd take his picture. Mini-me was wise for his age. Only one gator ever topped the size of the deceased predator. We were playing Oyster Bay in Sunset beach, N.C., a virtual gator playground. Gator counting almost trumped our score tallying each time we played the land occupied by swamp creatures. We once had to hold our ground on the tee box as a seven-footer crossed from one lake to another twenty yards in front of us. I still have that video. While on that tee box, another gator sneakily swam close by to our right. Other gators glided here and there on the lake. As we maneuvered the cart path, same hole, an explosion of fury in the water to our left prompted us to floor the gas peddles on our electric carts. Be berry, berry quiet, I think it was mating season.

Oyster Bay Tee Box Gator
(An eight-footer playing through in front of tee box)

The granddaddy of them all sunned itself on the green ahead.
Godzilla was on the edge of the green. Thankfully the flag was
planted on the opposite side. The nightmarish creature's head was
massive; its jaw hinged wide open. I estimate it was three feet wide
and over twelve feet long. Robbie Lucas, of Eastern Indian origin,
and one in our threesome, approached the gator. What possessed him
to do defied logic. He was maybe twenty feet from it when it began
emitting a throaty growl. I warned him that gators can outrun people
on land for short distances. And, it was a short distance between him
and his obviously irritated foe. Robbie, undaunted or just plain
crazy, replied, "Gators don't like dark spicy food." Thankfully he
backed away heeding the disgruntled reptile. I guess I was so caught
up in the awe of the moment that I failed to snap a photo. Having
Robbie in the foreground would have made the perfect comparison.
The gator never flinched or closed its mouth as we putted out and
then exited the premises. Should have snapped a photo of this
Godzilla but didn't want one with Robbie as bait.

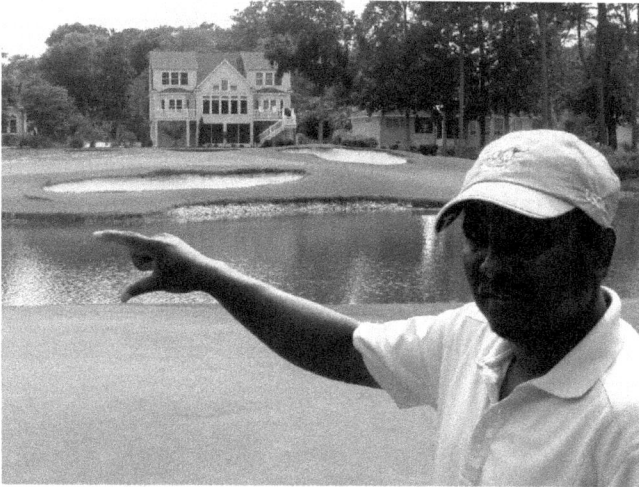

Robbie Lucas Pointing to another Large Gator in Oyster Bay Front Yard

Zoomed in Photo of Robbie's Gator

Eric, Tayla and I were playing the Heritage course in Pawley's Island. It's one of the Legends courses as is Oyster Bay. An enormous gator sunned itself near one of the greens. Using young Tayla as scale, keeping her a safe distance away, I did snap a photo of this giant water lizard. The Heritage always promises gator sightings. Sometimes they anchor the lakeshore along the number eighteen fairway ranging in lengths of three to well over ten feet long. I've counted as many as eight many times lined up along the lake's shoreline.

Tayla on the green with huge gator in right background

Gator without Tayla

98

(*No, the gator didn't get her.*)

Oh yeah. I must mention that we stopped at the turn at the Heritage during this round and ventured inside the club house for a potty break and for Eric and Tayla to grab some lunch. I had just retrieved my sandwich from my golf bag and placed it in the cart. Upon our return I discovered that my sandwich, Ziploc and all, had vanished. Prime suspect, one of those mutated elves must have snatched my lunch. I don't think gators have evolved into accomplished golf cart thieves yet. Tayla told me not to worry, she would make me lunch next time.

The Witch Golf Course in Conway has a huge gator owning the wetlands on the back nine. It's something about gators and sunning near greens. The king of the Witch trolls for wayward putters apparently. I had never seen any gators on the Tupelo Bay Executive Course in Surfside until after the floods produced by Hurricane Florence in 2018. Now a three-footer has taken up residence and moves from pond to pond there. The funniest thing I witnessed was a pair of mallards shadowing this gator along the bank, quacking their bills off. When the gator moved, they followed, making it known that they didn't appreciate its presence in their backyard.

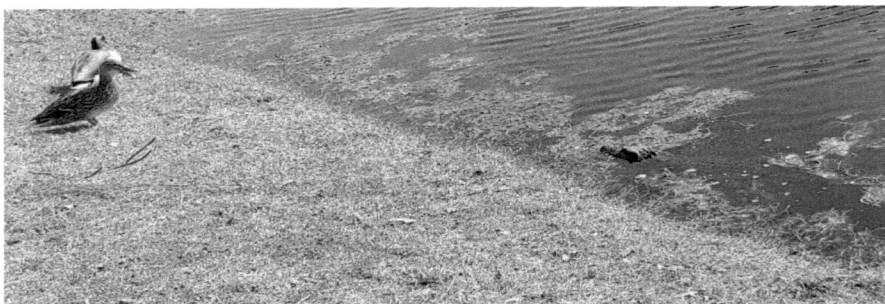

Mallards to the left and Gator on the Right

Tupelo Bay Gator near Egret

Gators are common and territorial in the water hazards. I once read that an alligator would travel up to a mile over land to the next waterway. Sandpiper Golf Course in Sunset Beach, North Carolina, not far from Oyster Bay was home to some impressive gators. We spotted them sunning in the backyards of homes and along the edges of the greens. The gentleman loading our bags on the carts issued a stiff warning for us to not linger long on the edges of the water hazards seeking lost golf balls. It was better for us to drop another ball and forget the lost one. I kidded Tom from West Virginia who was persistent in finding his ball in the water's edge, to wait until I engaged the video on my cell phone, not wanting to squander the attack from beneath. He promptly gave up his search after that comment.

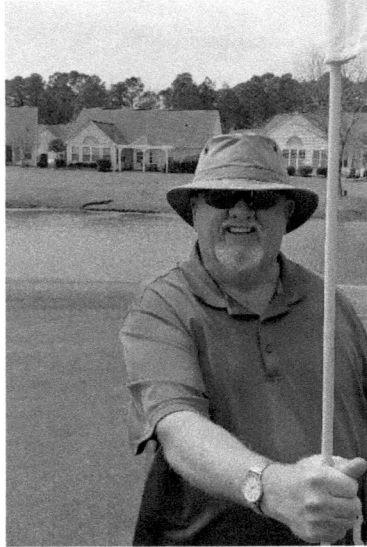

West Virginia Friend Tom Marsh
(Gator on lawn over his left shoulder at Sandpiper Bay)

Close up of Gator from Previous Photograph
(Imagine coming outside and seeing this.)

Huge Gator Greenside at Sandpiper Bay
'Putt out quickly!'

It's the gators you don't see until the last possible moment that can send chills rippling down your spine. Luckily for us, the gators don't seem too interested in golfers as appetizers. Most will swiftly shimmy into the water if you get too close. I try not to get too close myself. No ball or photo opt is worth it. When I do take photos, I utilize the telephoto lens instead. Up close is not too close using this option. Ah yes, I've seen more gators than I can tally for the past fourteen years living along the Carolina coast. Some gators have even ended up on the beaches. Luckily, we weren't sunbathing at the same time. Up until our move here, the only gators I had seen up close and personal were in zoos and the infamous gator farms in Florida. It puts a different spin on the situation when the mighty lizards are encountered in the wild. Golf courses weren't where I would have expected to see them though. *Being berry, berry quiet is advised.*

Sneaky Gator along edge of Oyster Bay Fairway

Ed Menamin takes on gator challenge at Tupelo Bay, his ball resting uncomfortably close to the reptilian hazard just left of flag. Marvin Jose, in the background, rewards Ed with Gator Ball Trophy for completing the challenge in one piece and launching his shot across the water ono the green. Ball was yellow with a green gator stamped on it.

Less intimidating, the Cooters are on almost every beach course water hazard

A funny sight on one of the tee boxes at the Indigo Creek Course is how the cooters will exit the water and approach golfers. Sometimes there will be as many as a dozen inching their way close the cart. These little fellers are apparently accustomed to handouts. We usually toss them some crackers. Unlike feeding squirrels or racoons, the cooters aren't fast enough to stalk you and they can't climb in the golf carts and steal you blind.

The Golf Planner

Assuming responsibilities for planning golf outings introduces many liabilities and poses more obstacles than planning a wedding. You'd think this would be a simple task, but you'll never find your golfing buddies lined up, bickering over who'd like to set up that next tee time. Each of us that have tried have gotten burned more times than we can fudge strokes on a score card. The unpredictable human behavioral habits leave few opportunities for mulligans or do-overs.

First hurtle when planning that next tee time is commitment. Know your no shows. Historically, who can you depend on to be there? Be leery of the flip-flopper. The "I'll let you know" response then you are following that up with numerous "are you in or out" inquiries should send up warning flags, especially if you're approaching the eleventh hour for calling to make that tee time.

Mr. No Show may or may not let you know they won't make the tee time. Too often you'll discover this at the course when you must return to the club house to pick up the starter ticket. He has your cell number, but you end up calling him and he rattles off, "It was raining at my house" and you're searching the heavens for a cloud in the sky. Or he whines, "something came up", interpreted, *my wife wouldn't let me play.*

Shooting for a foursome and getting a fivesome or thinking you have a foursome and number five showing up can stress you out, your RSVP fellow golfers and the golf course staff. The course makes you divide into a twosome and threesome with none wishing to play with the fifth wheel, or they allow the fivesome then all must contend with a snail's pace round. It's ugly, ugly, ugly and not within your control to reconcile.

We all have our favorite courses and those we loath. Remember, you're the designated planner so pick one you like. They can pick if they choose to plan. The starting time is the trickier of the two choices. I, for one, don't prefer to play early. Not because I can't rise and shine; I just hate wet dewy fairways. Others hate afternoons, especially during the summer when the heat and humidity kick in. Hot dry conditions assist my ball roll. Making everyone happy will be a problem.

Kitchen passes. Assist your buddies in acquiring permission from the significant other when possible. Or maybe it is wiser and safer to stay out of this one.

League play, now here's where I prefer not being the planner. Some people refuse to play with other people. So petty. No shows are prevalent as commitment is just a word. Challenges. Who is playing 9 holes? Who's playing 18? Who is teeing off first? Are we doing closest to a pin? Who is keeping the money for closest to the pin? Are we playing our ball or are we doing Captain's Choice? Just show up and we'll figure it out seems to be the way this usually goes

Tournament play, no way will I plan this one! Same above problems times ten. All were gathered at Burning Ridge course for a morning round. The groupings had been defined and everyone headed to the first tee box. Phone rings after first groups had begun their round. Caller asks. "Where's everybody?" He's at the wrong course. He shows up in time to now make the last group a fivesome. How did that go you ask? Not too good! The foursome is pissed and to add injury to insult, player number five is spraying his ball all over the course and can't seem to keep track of where it lands. This makes for a lovely day.

Bachelor weekends are yours to plan. Your fellow whompers should rally to support your choice of courses, tee times, days of play as you will return the favor when they have that all-inclusive Kitchen Pass weekend.

Beware taking on the role of Substitute Golf Planner in any of the above scenarios. One incident comes to mind. Our would-be substitute planner decided not to follow the template established by the primary planner for the company's weekly golf outing. Interpreting his e-mail to those scheduled to play: *I'll wait for no one. You're basically on your own. I know who I'm playing with and will already be on the course by the time you arrive. I'm above*

collecting money and keeping up with these silly little games of
chance (closest to the pin). Be careful out there, and have a good
time, whether you want to or not! If you have any complaints, you do
the planning next week.

I assumed this role once for same company outing. I too e-mailed the
participants the groupings and defined a plan B for no shows, and,
too, declined the closest to the pin option. Plan A nor B worked due
to the no-shows. We winged plan C, realigned the groups and no
causalities were reported after the round. Sometimes, even I can
blindly find that acorn.

The Golfer's Kitchen Pass

One can not play a round of golf if one cannot make it to the golf course. Oh, how often does the avid golfer or striving Whomper attempt to justify to a spouse, a significant other, parents or the boss why they should be allowed to play that beloved round of golf. You must be creative to ensure success or be prepared to pay the consequences when these explanations don't hold water. If you're a golfer you've been there and will most assuredly find yourself there again. Sometimes your little schemes have worked. Other times they have been doomed from the beginning. You probably stammered and stuttered, failing to execute. The perfect golfing kitchen pass must flow effortlessly from that golden tongue of yours.

You ask why you could possibly need a pass. Why not sneak off secretly to that round with the buds? Guaranteed, you most certainly will shoot that personal best low round, break some type of club record or sink the elusive hole in one. Secure your kitchen pass first and then celebrate guilt free and openly.

From the pages of the Golfer's Kitchen Pass Manuel, here are some of my favorite passes:

Invite her family to visit. Make sure there is a golfer among them. Take that in-law for a round allowing her quality time with her non-playing relatives.

Invite your family for same reason as above, however, it is important that you ensure she's compatible with yours before you strand her with them.

"It's a company tournament and it would look bad to my superiors if I didn't participate. Besides, it's free golf."

"It's a Vendor treat. It doesn't cost me to play today and its part of the job."

"This is my fourth round on my local's pass. I'll receive a free round next time I play."

"This is my free round on my local's pass."

"But honey, Angie and Marianne are letting John and Carl play this afternoon. Now how would it look if I didn't join them?"

"Fred's wife is out of town for the weekend and we're obliged to keep him occupied because you know how he has that wild streak. We're playing Saturday and Sunday to keep him out of trouble."

Parlay Mother's Day into a kitchen pass. "Just for you on your special day, let's do an early brunch (your choice of restaurants). Afterwards, I'll take the kids or grandkids and/or son-in-law golfing. Relax, do what you want to do on me and enjoy some quiet time alone with your daughter."

Pick a vacation spot with a golf course, all inclusive with the green fees or free rounds of golf included. Guilt free golf guaranteed, especially if you treat her to the spa.

Pick one of those plus 90-degree days: "Honey, would you go with me to the course today? I know you don't like to play but it'll only take four or five hours of your time." Pick a rainy day or day of greater than 50% rain predicted and ask same as above. Pick a cold day and you know the drill. She'll gladly let you play without her.

Have one of your buds call your house to ask if you could join him. Make sure you know when he plans to call and let your significant other answer the phone. Trust me, they will not say no. Typical answer: Doesn't matter to me or he does what he wants. Grab the clubs and exit the building quickly, Elvis!

"Gerald has a two for one pass, so he's letting me split the cost with him."

Go shopping with her or do something that isn't your cup of tea. Hopefully this can be later parlayed into a golf outing.

112

Encourage your wife to go out on an afternoon with the girls. It will help justify that day of golf with the boys. Better still, have the wife invite some of her girl friends over for the weekend. It gives you an excuse to get out of their way. Even better, encourage her to go visit the girl friends for the day or weekend. Free golf if you do not give her the opportunity to develop a "honey do list" of projects for you.

Kitchen Pass Tip: Remember you may strategically utilize *the sad puppy dog look.* Tilt your head slightly, squint or partially close your eyes and then have that slight whimper in your voice as if in submission. Lip quivering is not a bad touch. Do not try this unless you have practiced and perfected it. While projecting, ask can if you can play a round with the boys.

The *"I can't help you pass"* - You've been out of town on business for a few days and your flight returns at 11 AM Sat morning. Your buds are playing at noon. Decision, do you go straight from the airport and join them on the tee box or go home first? You're on your own on this one. If your marriage or relationship is on the rocks and you're looking to put that final nail in the coffin then by all means tee'em up, if you're looking for that perfect ending to launch you into a life alone.

Off Limits: Christmas, Thanksgiving Day, Valentines Day, her birthday, anniversaries, graduations, family funerals, if she's sick, if she's in the hospital, non golfing family or friends visiting.

The Kitchen Pass Creed

I, *your name*, swear to execute the appropriate golfer's kitchen pass, delivering an academy award performance, and leading by example for those less fortunate. I shall maintain my integrity as I overcome insurmountable odds ensuring my spot on the round's final four. I shall encourage my playing partners to support each GKP with the same vigor, conviction and sincerity as I so that they will never be doubted by those expected to grant them. To protect the GKP manual, I must not abuse the passes and will not divulge the manual's existence to those grantors of the pass. I will enjoy the round guilt free and encourage others to do the same.

Blame it on Ken

Ken has been such an intricate part of the coastal golfing group that I had almost forgotten how he stumbled into our inner circle. Carl Vigstedt first introduced us to Ken. Ken brought game to our group. Unfortunately, not golf game. Still, Ken had extraordinary charisma and eventually won us over. Now, he often rounds out our foursome or graces us with his presence as the fifth wheel. Ken is the focal point for many of the shenanigans that haunt our group. You can always count on good ole Kenny boy to help tone down even the toughest round of play with his antics. I'm not sure how we survived a round without him.

On many of the more challenging courses we play, our recruit, Ken, is deployed ahead of our foursome to strategically relocate the tee markers to improve our driving opportunities. There's only one problem with sending him ahead. Ken has this squirrel fetish and it tends to distract him from his mission. We have those huge fox squirrels populating the courses here on the Grand Strand, not like those puny little grey ones back home in Abbeville. My grandpa would have been in seventh heaven with these *big'uns* as he would have called them. There'd be enough dumplings to go around for the whole neighborhood after bagging just two or three. Better watch my mouth; Ken doesn't tolerate us disrespecting his friends, his fury tailed kingdom.

One of my favorite Ken episodes occurred at The Witch golf course near Conway. We had a morning tee time, all arriving early except Carl and Ken. Ken really enjoys riding in Carl's convertible so I'm sure they were probably taking the longer route to the course that beautiful sunny spring morning. He's worse than a dog with an open car window. Carl allows Ken to take advantage of him; just one man's opinion.

After signing in and paying for our round, we informed the young lady at the desk that Carl and Ken should be arriving shortly. They could catch up with us on the putting green. We warned her that Ken could be a little eccentric and Carl was just a tad on the obsessive-compulsive side. Tad is a southern term, not golfing lingo. Carl is not a southerner, but we still allow him to play in our foursome. He's originally from Vermont or one of those snow ravished states; a fir piece from the palmetto state. Fir is not a tree as used in this context.

Upon arriving ten minutes later, the desk attendant greeted Carl and commented how glad she was to see that Carl had brought Ken along. She informed them where they could find us. Carl and Ken arrived at the putting green, Carl is puzzled that she recognized both him and Ken. He recapped the incident in detail, smelling a rat. Fred Kane, John Schwindel and I busted a gut laughing. Carl asked how she knew about Ken, convinced that they had never previously met. Ken had never played The Witch, so he certainly didn't remember ever seeing her. We had to confess. Carl nodded; he didn't think she'd ever laid eyes on Ken before and if she had, she could have had him confused with someone else. Ken didn't exactly stand out in a crowd.

Well, to set the record straight, Ken is Carl's imaginary friend. If recollection serves me, Ken became the default name for one of Carl's friends when he couldn't remember people's names. He'd greet everyone as Ken figuring it'd be better than asking them to repeat their names. Carl shared this story with us, and a legend was born. We began addressing each other as Ken on the tee box, at the snack bar and so forth then Ken eventually evolved into an actual entity. We started blaming Ken for selecting the wrong club for us, driving the cart poorly, talking while we putted or just generally disrupting our rounds. Ken could be counted on to pencil whip a false score on the card. I sure made a lot of bogeys when Ken kept our score. By the way, bogeys are a good thing when we're talking my golf game.

"Where's Ken?" could be heard throughout our rounds. Ken became our *Harvey the Rabbit* from the *Jimmy Stewart* classic movie. We can visualize Ken doing almost anything and we rarely play a round without him. Matter of fact, Ken coauthored this article. He's quite the story spinner. Blame him for the editing.

One side note, Carl also has another friend, possibly his alter ego, Wayne. Carl and I were attending a Super Bowl party with friends at a local bar and grill. The waitress kept calling Carl, Wayne every time she dropped by to check on us. Apparently, Wayne picked up our bar tab because we never saw one. For the record, Wayne is not a golfer. He never joins us for outings. I don't think he and Ken get along. You can usually find Wayne tagging long at the bar though. He hasn't picked up any tabs lately.

Excuse me now. I must go. I've been informed that Ken has cornered the beverage cart lady again and will not allow her back in her cart until she gives him some goobers for the squirrels. That's peanuts for you non-southerners. "Ken, leave the young lady alone and go move those white tees on number five up like we asked you to do. And Ken, no squirreling around this time, please, or you'll be banned from riding in the convertible! I do believe our dear Kenny just flipped me the finger."

Keep your round honest out there. You never know when Ken may be watching. He's such a blabber mouth. Next round is on Wayne, by the way. Where's Carl?

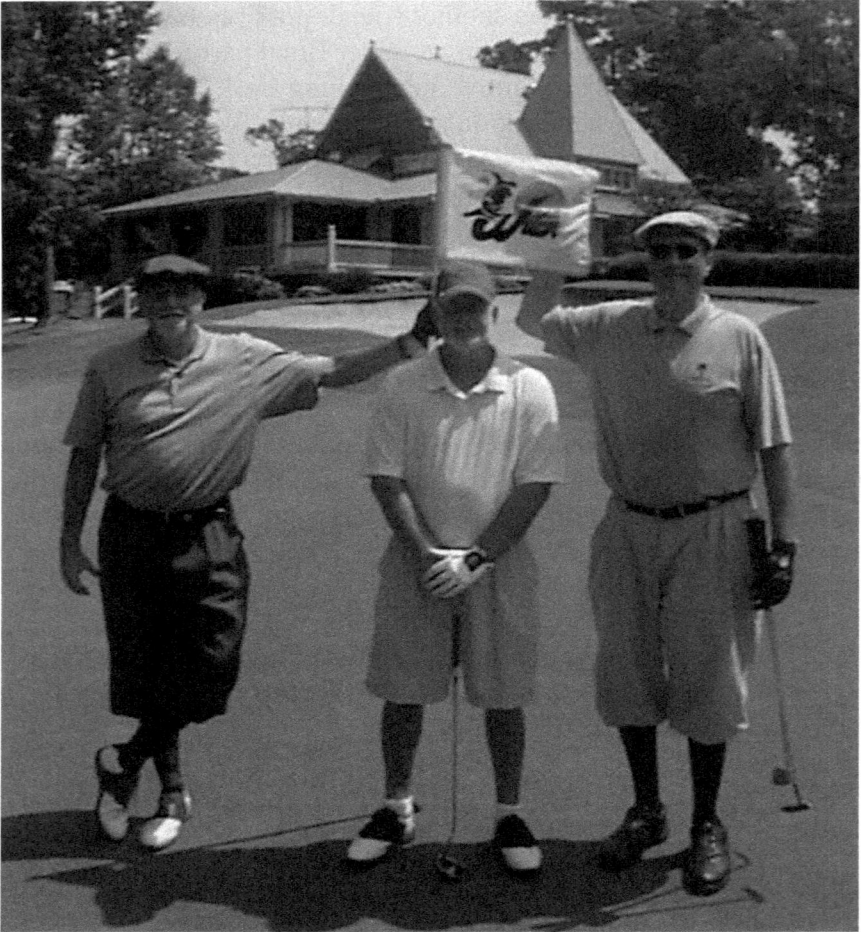

Witch Golf Course, Conway, S.C.
(*From left to right: Me, Ken, Carl and Fred*)
Either Wayne or John snapped this photograph.

O.C. Call Home

What's worse on a golf course than a cell phone? Answer: A highly obsessive-compulsive buddy with a cell phone playing in your foursome. And, you ask, what's worse than an OC using a cell phone in your foursome? Answer: A second anal retentive member of your foursome reacting to the OC's use of the phone. And what's worse than two OC's in the same foursome? Answer: Making the mistake of allowing both in the same golf cart.

What began as a lovely morning on Murrell's Inlet Blackmoor Golf Course soon took an ugly dark twist? Again, what were we thinking, allowing these two under-medicated characters, Carl and Fred, as cart buddies? We should have learned our mistake during the previous pairings when the two lingered over a twenty foot putt for about ten minutes squatting and stalking the hole while debating the break, the speed, the distance, the wind velocity and direction, the required putter velocity, the air temperature, the green temperature, the water temperature, humidity, alignment of the planets, their zodiac signs, what each had for breakfast, brand of golf ball being used, the number of dimples on the golf ball, the meaning of life, medication preferences, the feeding patterns of the local turtles and the general disposition of the squirrels on the course before they finally missed the putt.

Most of us either set our phones on vibrate or leave them in our automobiles, but not our OC pal, Fred. This technology must not be squandered nor taken lightly. Failure to maintain communication with the universe could ultimately lead to the world's destruction if the amazing OC is not there to save the day. He began receiving incoming calls almost immediately and we soon realized the developing pattern and would be caller would not take, "I'm busy, dear," as an answer.

The mistress of the house relentlessly made contact just because she was empowered to do so. Sounded like the little woman must be providing play by play updates of her morning's activities and how he could impact their outcome. Sadly, our OC pal did not keep these conversations private, blasting out his responses as if he were the only golfer within in ears shout on the course. He talked, we listened, whether we cared to or not.

Now anyone who plays golf knows that the tee box is sacred ground. Only very low whispers are permissible. Refraining from talking while your fellow competitors hit their balls should be the rule, not the exception. Oblivious, he didn't realize how disruptive these little one-way conversations could be. He continued his discussions with the little lady from the comfort of his cart while others attempted to strike their balls on the tee boxes or in the fairways.

One phone call, we give you a pass. Second call, a little more annoying, we roll our eyes and sneer. Third call, we are now regretting we invited you and thinking bodily harm. Forth incoming call, now bordering on ridiculous, it is dangerous to have our hands on a club. The remaining three begin visualizing how far we think we could drive your phone. By call number five, the group is livid. Now throwing caution to the wind, we watch, we wait for our first opportunity to snatch this little communication device and pay homage to the water gods at the next hazard. We are no long your friends! Be afraid, be very afraid!

Our anal-retentive partner, Carl, has now lost a sense of reality, unable to focus on both his game and the phone conversations taking place from his co-rider. He stands on the tee box and addresses his ball while glancing over his shoulder begging for the madness to stop. First attempt, his ball dribbles ten yards off the tee box. Yelling, 'Do-over,' he turns and gives *the still talking loudly* Fred an *I must kill you* jeer. Regaining his composure, he tees up and strikes a second ball with similar results. The do-over cry rings in our ears once again. Now he's livid. We're expecting him to go into mortal combat with our disruptive *soon to not be* friend. Carl successfully launches the third attempt as Fred finally ends his call.

Still unfazed, he nonchalantly comments he that should have probably left his phone in the car. Confirming that it would be a wise decision, we elaborate. (A) We will take possession of his phone in the parking lot next time (B) If OC fails to allow us to assist him then we'll have no choice but to introduce him to the versatility of the latest technology; it can be used for an enema, his, (C) How is it on impact and is it waterproof? Or (D) We'll answer the phone and whisper, 'Honey, I'll meet you at our usual rendezvous spot', and then confiscate it and place it on silent mode. Golf buddies are priceless. Toleration is an accomplished skill.

Pal, John had a different spin on life golfing with Fred. He turned to something more leisurely relaxing. This is John's take and newfound pastime.

Why Crabbing is more fun than Golfing with Fred

• They won't argue yardage distance
• You can eat the crab and not the golf ball
• They don't heckle you in your backswing
• You only pay attention to the tides and not the grain in the grass
• They don't drink your beer
• They don't debate what club to use
• You don't have to wait until 2 PM

Calling Sigmund Freud

As already declared, we are so fortunate to have obsessive compulsive behavior among us...not. The term is often used to describe a person deemed to be overly obsessed with minor details and having such attention to detail that the obsession becomes an annoyance to others. Yep, that's him alright. Carl refers to himself as a bit on the quirky side. We concur. This makes for interesting golf, especially for the lucky one who co-pilots the cart with him. Usually that duty falls on my shoulders. While entertaining at times, it can also contribute to slower pace, a taboo on the course.

Each round starts with his pre-game warm up, extending both arms and rotating them as if preparing to take flight. I'm not sure how this exercise prepares one for hitting the golf ball, but I guess it rotates his rotator cuffs. Could be preventive measures to ensure he doesn't seize up during the round. Now if the weather is borderline cold, this can prompt the apparel cycle syndrome. He starts by wearing the jacket or pullover on the first tee. It may be removed and replaced countless times during the round. 'Clap on, clap off, clap on, clap off.' Slower play, yes, you may bet the bank on it. When my wife has this problem, I refer to it as being unable to regulate her thermostat. Speaking of weather, when it rains, we must flip down the built-in bag hood provided on most carts. This introduces too may challenges for my cart buddy. He can be heard struggling with it as if he were wrestling with a twenty-foot tarp. Sounds like he's losing his match.

Whomper rules, we allow one mulligan per nine to be used any time during the round. Most of us save our mulligans for those tough holes or after we really botch up a shot. Not anal-boy, he will burn his mulligan early. Example, he worm burns a one hundred yard shot straight down the middle and then drops the mulligan and strikes it to repair his psychologically bruised ego. What a waste of a mulligan! More times than not, this decision comes back to haunt him later in the round. We get to say we told you so. But then he might declare a do-over, justifying that a do-over is not a mulligan.

He utilized the endless mulligan or do-over clause. I haven't found that one in the Whomper Rule Book yet.

Golf club management takes on a whole new meaning. Me, I just grab a club from the bag and return it by chunking it in any available slot, often requiring me to force it into the bag. My cart buddy, however, must replace the club head cover and strategically insert the club into a specific designated location. This task becomes more difficult and time consuming if replacing multiple clubs and a putter. Once I hear that familiar bag rustling sound over my right shoulder, it's a sure sign that he's in the middle of an anile episode.

Cleanliness to the OC inflicted, not a pretty sight. I use the towel to swipe at my clubs if I remember to do it before chunking them in the bag. Carl meticulously buffs each club to remove every blade of grass and smudge of dirt. I curse the courses that mount those ball and club washers on the cart because now it's like having a mobile laundry mat on board. Mostly when you're teeing off is when you hear that familiar swoosh and plunging sound emitting as you're trying to focus on your shot. Oblivious to his surroundings, he cleans with reckless abandon. Oh, and don't let him get any dirt, mud, blood, grass or hotdog stains on his attire. This will send him over the edge as he attempts to clean his clothing. I'm expecting him to start bringing a change of clothing.

My anal-retentive buddy often insists on driving the cart because he must be in control. The round is all about him. It's not uncommon for him to drive off and leave me standing in the middle of the fairway either with the wrong club or no club. Lost in the land of OC, he'll park conveniently by his ball, but I must walk to wherever my ball has landed or to the cart if I need a club change.

Cell phones. Enough said, I've already covered this in a previous chapter with OC partner number two, Fred. Carl reminds us not to confuse his disorder with Fred's. He says Fred's is far more advanced and obsessive than his. Fred will pick up cigarette butts, candy wrappers and things I don't care to mention when he spots them on the golf course or any place that occupies his space.

Then there is putting. Reaching the green poses more potential OC moments. Where do I start? Marking his ball, he leaves both the marker and his ball to mark the spot. This may be more of a senior moment than an OC one. His turn to putt and he drifts hopelessly in an anal hot air balloon, unaware that we're waiting for him to putt his ball. Never fails, he putts for a *gimme* then either walks in our line or stands in the line as it is all about him, his green, his moment, his world.

One episode stands out. We call it THE PUTT. I briefly mentioned this in previous chapter. Carl has a good round going but friends are always there for you. Fred does like his adult beverages, so let's just magnify anal retention just a tad. Fred decides to assist Carl with a twenty-foot birdie putt on the 17th at Blackmoor. How'd that go you ask. *Not too good!* They stalked the hole from every possible angle taking turns squatting behind one another discussing the speed, the break, the stroke, grain of the green, the wind direction, the humidity, the temperature, wind chill, heat index, the alignment of the stars, aches and pains, favorite beverages, the meaning of life, the origin of man, heaven and hell, what's your sign. There was no bet or record-breaking round hinging on their decision to do this. For the record, Carl missed the putt. Eric and I had already putted out and were sitting in the cart. We called the clubhouse to enquire if a therapist might be on the course. As if choreographed, the dynamic OC duo screeched in disbelief as the putt skewed left and short.

Fear not, these anal antics can be countered. Well, maybe not countered but one can get inside the head of the *anal-retentive* bud. Rearranging the clubs in the bag without him knowing it is a favorite. Switch club head covers. Keep scratching through scores on the card, scribbling corrections. Unzip pockets on their golf bag. Pile your empty cans and trash in the basket behind him. Point out a dirty spot on their clothing (best on their backside so they can't verify it.) Walk or stand briefly in *their* putting line. Cough then accidentally take a swig of their beverage. Tell them their golf ball is dirty. Never let them complete a sentence. Comment that you noticed something different in their swing, stance, grip or height they are teeing up their ball. Shake your head after they swing and say, "You did it again." Don't tell them what you meant by the comment.

It is fun rattling the cages of my OC buddies. Sending them into an obsessive frenzy is priceless. I shouldn't be boasting about it though. They can't seem to help it. I certainly can. There is but one obvious solution. "Sigmund Fraud, would you be our fifth?"

La-La Land

Have you ever had one of those rounds where your playing partners seemed to struggle with why they were on the course? Their mission to be a distraction overshadowed the round. You soon asked yourself, what was I thinking when I asked them to play? I'm a Whomper so my game can't be subjected to too many distractions or my score will soar upward into the triple figure abyss. Let's explore a few personal experiences and you determine if they sound familiar.

In-laws, some call them a necessary evil, saying you either love them or must keep reminding yourself that you're supposed to love them. In my case, I do love my extended family. That being established, here's the first scenario. My brother-in-law Raymond and son-in-law Gene join me for an afternoon of golf at the Azalea Sands golf course. Neither plays golf that often. Have you ever met that person that you've asked, "what time is it?" and they tell you how to build the watch. Well now picture playing eighteen holes with two of them. They could pass for father and son, physically and personally, even though they aren't related. My bad, to make matters worse, I paired them in the same cart.

Fast forward, we're a threesome so we should play at a descent pace, right? Soon my two little philosophers/historians had drifted into their own fifth dimension, oblivious to their surroundings and foursome's now breathing down our backs. I'm an extremely laid-back person but my stress level redlined as I tried to cattle prod my beloved relatives along, trying to maintain a descent distance ahead of the pursuing golfers, patiently watching our play or lack thereof. Snails bolted out of their way as they carted the fairways. I swear the rough mimicked Kudzu growing an inch before my eyes. The unfolding scene reminded me of one of those dream sequences where slow motion frame by frame movements hampered every shot. I think the beverage cart passed us twice on one of the par fives. I must have aged at least a year in dog years. So, what was one to do to stop the bleeding?

By now we had allowed several foursomes to play through and the course patrons continued to log jam behind us. I constantly glanced over my shoulder waiting for the dreaded ranger to stop by and scold us for our sins. For reasons I can not explain, we were spared this embarrassment. The final straw came on a par four paralleling the local rural airport with small planes landing and taking off regularly. I had reached the green and my terrible two had finally joined me. I completed my putt and watched as they finally did the same. I walked off the green to my cart. In disbelief, I turned to see my extended family still standing on the green watching planes and in deep discussion. The foursome behind us stood impatiently in the fairway waiting for them to clear the green. There they stood though, undaunted in their private little world.

Breaking point reached, throwing up my hands, I yelled, "Guys haven't you ever seen a plane before?" I then pointed to the group behind them. With no great urgency, Twiddle-Dum and Twiddle-Dee ambled off the green, still immersed in their conversation. This never-ending story had no tortoise and hare ending. Moral never invite them to play at the same time. Can you divorce in-laws?

Scenario number two, I was playing with high school friend Mike and Cuz visiting us at the beach. Coworker Eric rounded out the foursome. The round came unraveled on the third hole at the Blackmoor golf club. Eric and I had parked our cart beside the green and headed with putters in hand to mark our balls. Bad decision, I had allowed Cuz and Mike to ride in the same cart. Remember that never worked for the OC boys. Scanning the fairway, we immediately noticed the two of them just standing there talking, no clubs in hand. The foursome behind stood cross-armed, contemplating the little situation as were we.

Eric turned to me and asked, "Have they not seen one another in a long time?" To which I responded, "They see one another all the time. I don't know what they're doing?" Now yelling and pointing behind them, they got the picture and eventually retrieved their clubs and struck their balls. Adult beverages most likely played a part in their game plan.

The yell, "Cold Beer!" could be heard throughout the round as Cuz and Mike kept better pace with their consumption of beer than the golf game. Silver lining, I did whip both of them.

Scenario three, never allow two obsessive compulsives to ride in same cart. No further recanting of round required. It's bad, very bad on all levels.

Scenario, four, taking young children and the son-in-law golfing at same time; expect more of the above.

Conclusion, know your partners or be prepared to face the music. Practice patience and remember golf clubs are not weapons. FFF (forced family fun) can be just that. Cold beer at 8 AM might not necessarily be a bad thing if you're the one consuming it. Become a traffic controller and wave those other groups through. Extend your deepest apologizes and tell them the club house just paired you with these strangers. Learn to smile and nod, drink more adult beverages than them. Try to complete the round with no causalities. Golf is just a game and the season is not over yet. Claim your back is out the next time any of them mention playing, even though the pain is lower. Divide and conquer, pairings in carts are important. Live to Whomp another day!

Hey Mr. Ranger, Where's Yogi?

The golf ranger on any given course typically oozes a persona, better or worse than the average bear, right, Boo-Boo? Mr. Ranger might be the timekeeper from hell, relentlessly reminding one's group to keep up the pace or he may possess excellent people skills making it simply a joy to play the course. I've experienced both Jekyll and Hyde in the ranger ranks.

A good starter sets the tone of the round ahead. He explains the course rules, the flag placements, which fairways to stay on the cart path, where the restrooms are located and if there is a beverage cart. Starters can be polite and funny or might be stone faced when reciting their spill. Once we're on the course Mr. Ranger is the enforcer of the rules. He completes the checks and balances after you depart the first tee box motoring counterclockwise on the course, same as the beverage cart. Why not combine these jobs and call her the Rescue Ranger? She can cater to your needs and ensure that you are compliant with the rules and speed of play. Seems a two-for would be more practical and economical.

As mentioned, Mr. Ranger's main objective is to keep us moving. Quipping 15 minutes per hole as he passes, he encourages us to speed up play. I almost always have at least one anal retentive player in my group, and sometimes two. Sorry, 15 minutes isn't going to happen. We were instructed by Mister Ranger during a recent round to speed it up when the group behind us trailed us by at least 1 ½ holes. Mr. Ranger, I fear, sometimes just had to feel his oats. Oh yeah, and what are you writing on that clipboard of yours? Becoming frustrated with slow play because of the group ahead of us, we corralled Mr. Ranger Sir during his next drive by and complained. He stated he could do nothing because they were course members and always played slow. *If things got any slower, we'd be an eight-some.* There are exceptions to The Rules, the membership clause #3.2.1. The beverage wench reinforced our wear-it-on-our-sleeves aggravation on her next round stating, "Bless your hearts guys, you're behind them. They hold up everyone. May I offer you an adult beverage to offset your stress?"

One of the nicer courses we have played, The Myrtle Beach National, Kings North, has huge Big Ben clocks mounted on post at every tee box to help pace your round. Kind of like those signs stating *You Are Here*. Do they really work? Not without Mr. Ranger riding rough shod. It sounds like we always play slowly. We really don't most of the time. And most of the time the rangers are cordial and often kidders.

During a round at Island Green Golf Course we complained about the group playing ahead of us being too slow. They were playing from the furthest tee box, the blue tees and were worse hackers than us and we were playing from the Whites. Our comments immediately triggered flash backs from Mr. Ranger, and he shared a story from a recent round. A previous Blue Man Crew hacked their way from one tee box to the next. Observing this phenomenon, Mr. Ranger intercepted them on the next tee box and abruptly explained the terms of their continued play.

"If you can't strike the ball any better than that off the blues, move up to the whites and you better be on the whites when I make my next round. If you suck there too then I'm moving, you to the gold tees. Flounder there and the Reds are all that's left for you guys. That will require a quick surgical procedure that I am both obligated and qualified to perform on each and every one of you. Now, please enjoy the course and have fun, but do it at a speed that others will appreciate."

Mr. Ranger approached, never gave an inch and forced both our carts off the cart path to avoid a head on. Nodding, he passed as if we were the lowest on the food chain. Guess what Mr. Ranger, we're paying customers. Why should we move out of your way? Cart path only apparently only applies to Mr. Texas Ranger, Sir, and we were forced to utilize the 90-degree rule. Hindsight, we had two carts to his one and should have played chicken with him. By the way, why didn't you warn us about that twelve-foot gator in the pond on that last par three? That would have been valuable information.

The rangers are always trying to get more of my money with these Par Three contest. They wait near the tee box and tell us how we can earn rewards with a price of course. Hit the green and double your money. Doubling your money interpreted; we'll give you Monopoly money to purchase merchandise from the club house. No second mortgage required on any purchases. First, I haven't hit anything green all day unless you count that green townhouse on number twelve. My earnings wouldn't equate to the purchase of a bag of tees. Why don't you just give me a sleeve of balls and let's call it even?

Why aren't there any rangers on a Par Three golf course? Speed is a bigger deal because you're walking most of these. And believe me, some folks are not built right to walk nine holes carrying their clubs or pulling them. I can almost hear him yelling, *"Hey fat boy, you're going to have to pick up that pace or we're going to have to restrict you to the putting green!"*

Driving ranges; where are the Rangers. What's a range without a ranger? What would life be with Mr. Ranger riding the range? *"If you can't hit the ball further than ten feet, you're forfeiting that bucket to the next paying customer. Hit one more condo and you're banned for life, buck-a-roo. No, you can't retrieve those balls. Tee pad only! 90-degree rule, do not, I repeat, do not hit your fellow practicing mate."*

Mr. Ranger, there's a Jelly Stone Park Resort out there somewhere screaming your name. And I heard him exclaim as he made his rounds, *"Sorry, no pick-a-nic baskets allowed on the course, slows down the play"*.

Golfing with a Southern Belle

Arriving as a threesome at Myrtle Beach's Arrowhead Golf Course on a simply gorgeous Saturday afternoon, we soon had our fourth spot plugged by a genuine Georgia Peach. Originally from Atlanta, she had recently relocated to our beach resort town. After the formal introductions had been conducted, the boy members rose to the occasion, infected with a case of foot in mouth disease. We shared our sarcastic wit, part of the required curriculum for our group.

Our southern belle had drawn the short straw and had ended up in the cart with me. I inserted the first foot when jesting that I'd play from the red tees with her, assuming that all women played from the lady's tee. She quickly made it perfectly clear saying, "Red tees? I'll be playing from whatever tees that you gentlemen are playing?"

Gentlemen! How dare her! There are no gentlemen in our group. We conceded that it would help keep the round moving if we all played from the same tee box, even if it took her a couple of extra shots here and there to keep pace with us. We'd be playing our regular tee box, the white tees.

A second member of our little merry band broke it off deep when he laughed, "Maybe you can give us lessons today."

She responded, "Not on my day off."

We let that one slide, conceding that she was just trying to be one of us. Quick comebacks, we like that in a fellow player, even though I sniffed something fishy about her statement. After the little lessons remark, our bud decided to tee off first, reinforcing that we were not gentlemen. Old lefty fired his first ball into the woods to the right. This would require a breakfast ball second shot. We allow two off the first tee for just this very reason. Shot number two replicated shot number one. Lefty encouraged our new partner to hit next. BAM! Two hundred plus yards along the right edge of the fairway. She had nailed a lucky shot, not bad for a girl.

132

Lucky, I don't think so. She pared that first par four and did the same on the next, a par five. I noticed her name printed on her fancy bag followed by the number 101. Stupidly I inquired if she gave lessons or something. She responded, "Yes, I have been doing it for sixteen years, started playing when I was 9 years old." Now I'm not the best judge of age but I placed her in her mid to late forties. She then explained that she had relocated from Atlanta to a local beach resort four months prior. Her goal was to play all 113 courses along the Grand Strand, and in four short months she had already played 41 of them.

A couple of holes later I got a whiff of a cigar. I knew that no one in our group smoked. Our little southern belle had fired up the stogie, ended up puffing her way through the remaining holes. Her favorite things to do on her day off were play golf or ride her bike. Now, we're not talking about the peddling kind like mine. She owned a 500 cc something or another. None of us boys owned a bike, except for the peddling kind.

She soon began entertaining the group with southern slang. I for one understood everything she said as I'm a born and raised southern boy from historical Abbeville, South Carolina. My two buddies are northern transplants, same name as that George Steinbrenner baseball team if you catch my drift. Rolling off her tongue, such sweet phrases as *pert near, over yonder, nice'un, right-cher, ayer-it-is,* brought goose bumps. I had to interpret for my Yankee buddies. I hit my ball over yonder and pert near hit the green. Nice'un was heard after a few of our shots. When asked where her ball marker was, she responded, right-cher. While looking for a lost ball, she pointed and said ayer-it-is. Addressing the three of us on the tee box she asked, "What's closer, a tad or a hair?" priceless!

One of my buds said he had lived down here for twelve years so how come folks still had him pegged as a northerner? Our southern belle explained. It's not like having a green card or earning a visa and you can't transfer citizenship. You're either born here or you're not. Oatmeal or Cream of Wheat can not be substituted for grits. We eat biscuits, not bagels. We say, how y'all; not how ya doing in that

Tony Soprano dialect. I was hanging on her every breath. She painted the canvas as I have often done.

She began stepping on my profession though. I pride myself on flag management. I excel at pinning the flag and maintaining it, so it doesn't flap in the wind. She beat me to the flag on every hole. Now, I'm not sure if she really wanted my job or if her shots were always closest to the pin guaranteeing that she reached it first. Just to rattle me, she even whipped it around behind me like a marching band's color guard as I putted the ball. I liked it. She had style.

On number fifteen, the ranger made the same mistake that I had made on the first tee box. Explaining a promotional give-away for hitting the par three green, he gave the yardage from the white tees then assumed she'd be playing from the reds. He began telling her that yardage when *Scarlet* cut him off in mid sentence, "I'm playing from the whites my dear man."

Skeptical, he responded, "You're playing from the whites?" and shook his head. Yep, I'm sure he displayed the same look as I had expressed on number one. She placed her shot less than six feet from the pin.

She cleaned our clocks that glorious golfing day; shooting something well under par. I truly enjoyed the golf clinic, being my first time playing with a professional or *fessional* as my pal Gerald likes to phrase it. She made only one bad shot all day and that shot landed in the water on the 17th. She scored her only bogey on that hole. That's the only time she expressed a tad of frustration; not to be confused with a hair.

Shaking hands after completing the 18th, she curtsied in southern belle fashion while blowing smoke from her cigar. She thanked us for putting up with her. I can't believe one of us didn't respond "Frankly my dear, I don't give a damn." Guess she rattled us enough to make us lose our edge. I pulled from the parking lot in my pick-up truck and like a true southern gentleman, yielded her the right of way. We exchanged hand waves, the southern belle and I, as she drove off into the sunset in her sporty red Mustang, cigar smoke drifting from the open window. We never crossed paths gain and we can only assume that she completed her goal, playing every course along the Grand Strand.

'Act helpless and confused when it's to your advantage;
never let them know how clever and capable you really are.'
Southern Belle

The Golf Streak

Sunday afternoon, Legends Golf Course, weather forecast a bit iffy at best, but three brave warriors of the links were determined to complete the prepaid round. Eric, Fred and I ventured onto the course at our designated tee time, oblivious to the meteorologist naysayer and weather warnings. Thunder rumbled in the distance as we teed it up on hole number one. Thunder in the distance is not a threat. Rumble on and keep your distance. Everything will be fine. We had prepaid one flat fee for three months of unlimited golf after 1 PM, 24/7, holidays included. The more we played pushed the average round lower. I was working my $13 round as math goes. Cheap golf is indeed priceless.

As we navigated our way down the fairways Mother Nature echoed her apparent disapproval of play on the Sabbath. I know, a bit melodramatic for a whomping the ball story but author discretion prevails, drama builds. Smart phone technology allows us to maintain a watch on the ever-changing weather conditions. Doppler radar images even allowed us to track any storms in the immediate area. Nothing forbidding caught our attention, so we pushed onward in search of pars and birdies, or maybe just bogeys and double bogeys in my case. Stay clear of the evil snowman (an eight on the scorecard) is my mantra. I call scoring a seven on a par four failing to plant the head on the neck. Ole Frosty knows me by first name.

Mother Nature rumbled again, voicing her disapproval of us being on nature's playgrounds. On the sixth hole as the heavens opened the floodgates, we decided to strategically park our two carts. Fred, Eric and I hunkered down under the tree canopy. Blowing rain continued to pelt us. Then…the lightning arrived in full fury. One asks where the safest place is during a lightning storm. Beneath trees doesn't seem to be the best option. Bolts do strike the highest points or so we tend to hear. Out on the open fairway doesn't seem a logical choice either. Trapped between a rock and hard place we waited it out, hopeful that it would slack up sooner instead of later. It didn't. For the next hour we were the lone survivors hoping luck was on our side. To worsen matters, Eric's and my cart didn't have a fold up windshield. It was missing. That just offered an extra entry way for the blowing rain.

Finally, after an hour the rain began to slow. The fairway adjacent to us resembled a riverbed. What to do? What to do? Once the rain had shifted to a light drizzle, we did what we needed to do. We resumed our round. I finished the hole with; you guessed it, a snowman. Over the next three holes we whacked our golf balls and then fished them from newly formed lakes, to relocate the next shot on higher, not necessarily drier ground. Even on the greens we had to reposition our balls to align a dry path with the hole. We thankfully completed the first nine. What should we do now? Of course, we began the second nine. We appeared to be the lone wolves on the links. After teeing off, a ranger approached us from the opposite direction, riding in the fairway instead of on the cart path as one would assume. He was waving his hands frantically. As he approached, he informed us that the course was closed because the greens were waterlogged. So, were we, so what? It would be at least an hour of drainage before play could continue. We were an hour and half from dusk. Game over, we called it a day. The protector of the fairways didn't seem to notice that the back of his cart was broken and digging a trench two feet wide in the ground. Dumbassness knows no boundaries even when the culprit is a course ranger.

Our (Eric, Fred and my) next attempt to play would come three days later, Wednesday afternoon at 5. We experienced a groundhog movie moment. We kept an eye on darkening skies while checking radar and the forecast on our smart phones. Radar indicated that the storm would skirt us. Smart phones are not as smart as we give them credit. Standing on the par three #7, a thunderous bolt of extremely close lightning got our attention. We pulled under the overhang of the bathroom facilities with another gent already parked there. We checked those smart phones again, and, after about ten minutes we decided we could probably finish the last two holes.

Undaunted and struck by our case of dumbassness, we indeed decided to try to finish the final two holes on the front nine. Made sense, we were heading towards the clubhouse. An elevated green and elevated lightning activity proved we had made an extremely poor decision. We could see the rain at the clubhouse and vicious lightning convinced us to backtrack to the bathroom facility at the number seven green. By then several more carts were hunkered down. Lightning popped on all sides of our supposedly safe haven. What made us think that it wouldn't make a direct hit? At least we were mostly dry; unlike our last time under those trees. The rain blew in one direction and then in the opposite direction. The lightning was just plain scary. Finally, after about thirty minutes, we decided to make a mad dash for it. Lightning still popping about didn't boost my confidence level on the decision. Miraculously, we made it back to the parking lot. In two attempts in three days we had finished sixteen holes total. Tomorrow would be a new day, a new tee time.

We (Fred, Jim, Robbie and I) arrived at the clubhouse on Thursday to darkening skies. Smart phone and the Weather Channel App pointed out that the worst of the storm would skirt us. Our tee time was fifty minutes away yet. Just before that deadline arrived the skies unleashed its fury once again. The front desk announced that all three courses were officially closed until we had a lapse of at least thirty minutes with no lightning strikes. It rained. It thundered. It flashed and streaked awesome lightning. How did that line go in the Perfect Storm? Just when they thought they had escaped Clooney looks over to Walberg and says, "She's not going to let us out." Three attempts at a round of golf in four days, our completed holes remained at sixteen. Persistent, we were not quite done yet. It was just time to try another Legends course on our three-month prepaid deal. Saturday we would venture from Myrtle Beach to Sunset Beach, North Carolina, the sister course, Oyster Bay. The forecast was about the same, 60% chance of rain. Another course another state, just perhaps we would be granted a reprieve.

Carl, Eric and I arrived under mostly sunny skies. Fred had bailed on us; hindsight, maybe a smarter man. Things were looking more in our favor. The weather disturbances appeared further south, across the border. Just perhaps this change of venue had been the right call after all. Hospitality at Oyster Bay is always exceptional. At check in the attendant asked me if I had purchased the meal plan (two beers and lunch) with my special. Honesty is the best policy. I admitted that I hadn't but decided to buy the five-dollar ticket. He says, "Glad to have you here; here, you can have a free meal ticket." Lady luck was on our side or at least mine. We eventually teed off under perfect conditions, overcast skies and lower humidity. Yep, today was our day.

It wasn't long before the skies began complaining in the distance. Thunder rumbled southward and the horizon grew darker. We pressed onward, figuring no way could this happen to us again, not in another state. The odds were in our favor, right? The rumbling continued as did our round. It appeared that the storms were skirting us and heading out to sea. Skirting had not worked well for us thus far. No mulligan needed this round so it seemed. Oyster Bay came with enough challenges. We certainly didn't need adverse weather conditions to handicap the round. We periodically checked the weather on the smart phones and so far, so good. We had made the turn, further than previous rounds. The skies darkened but nothing ominous approached the course. The storm clouds rained southwest of Oyster Bay.

Five holes to go, we pulled up to a short par three across the water. All three of us safely reached the green and then light rain began to fall. The wind kicked up out of seemingly nowhere. Before we parked greenside the first flash of lightning commanded our attention. We quickly putted out; me too quickly, four putting for a double bogey. Lightning began popping regularly and way too close for comfort. Options, risk backtracking to a restroom to wait it out or hightail it to the clubhouse. The popping lightning convinced us that hightailing it was the only option. We were a long way from the clubhouse but full throttle we shot past the foursome in the middle of the fairway ahead of us.

We quickly found ourselves in ground striking lightning on all sides. I felt like we were running a battlefield gauntlet, fleeing for our lives. It was that scary and worse, we were driving those carts into the teeth of the storm. This was one I didn't think we were going to win. I flinched frequently at nearby bolts and strikes. By the grace of the Man above we made it to the parking lot and began transferring our clubs to our cars. The popping lightning was relentless, and thunder was directly on top of us. I'm still not sure why or how we kept from being struck. Everyone had arrived solo so there would be no safety in numbers for the commute back to Myrtle Beach. Torrential rain unleashed, almost too hard for the windshield wipers and by the time I reached Calabash and then Little River just six miles away, the roadways were flooded riverbeds. I needed a boat instead of a car.

Our streak now stood at four. We had had finished 9, 7, 0 and 14 holes but we would live to play another one hopefully. Legends golf packages, priceless... right?

Octogenarians

The following is a Carl Vigstedt encounter. No, it did not include Ken or Wayne or any of us this time. Carl and his beloved wife were visiting the sunshine state of Florida, staying a week at the Golfing Hall of Fame in Saint Augustine. He had parlayed three kitchen passes while his wife kicked back at the condo; sweet! Playing solo posed a challenge for Mr. Anal Retentive because he'd have no control over who he'd be paired with for each of the rounds. He'd get over it. He'd be golfing after all, and that's what really mattered.

The first day the course grouped him with northerners. Being a transplanted one himself, they never suspected he now resided in South Carolina. They bonded and discussed northerner stuff which probably included complaining or making fun of southerners. Carl, straddling the fence, could go with the flow. You can be assured that deer hunting, nor bass fishing or racing surfaced as topics. I don't recall what he said he shot for the round but, who cares, he was golfing while on family vacation. He could have been forced into a week of FFF (*forced family fun*); however, his wife apparently had a weak moment and granted him three passes. What's up with that?

The next round, I recall the pairings were similar. Like the ever-present Canadian geese, they seem to migrate south to enjoy our greens and fairways. These two were a couple of Wise Guys from the Jersey area. I had visions of *Joe Piscopo's* Saturday Night Live skit, "I'm from Jersey. Are you from Jersey? I'm from Jersey too."

Nevertheless, Carl fulfilled the male bonding experience and exercised kitchen pass number two, feeling at home with more northerners. He claimed that he shot a descent round completing the second eighteen without seizing up. We poor working folks made our eight to five while he made his five on eight. Life doesn't always seem fair, but we'd manage to get in a round or two without him, so it evens out in the long run.

Kitchen pass number three offered up a new twist for Carl. Just for the record, let's clarify that he was a young fifty-nine at the time of this episode. They paired him with a couple of gentlemen well into their eighties. To round out the foursome, one of the elder statesmen had invited his sixty-something year old trophy wife to join him as his nonparticipating cart co-rider. She would be the official score keeper. The second gentleman had suffered a stroke and still didn't have complete control over one side of his body. Carl said this inspired him. He'd refrained from complaining about his little insignificant aches and pains. He hoped to one day live the life they had, still playing golf at a ripe old age.

Back home, Carl usually plays from the senior tees or, as he refers to them, as the Championship tee boxes. The Florida cartel would have none of this. His choice of tee box was instantly met with ridicule from his older partners who still played from the white tees. Guilt ridden and embarrassed, Carl reluctantly retreated to the whites, forfeiting his presumed rite of passage to tee them up from the yellows. If the old codgers were game, so was he. His two partners encouraged the kid to tee off first. Reluctant at first, Carl finally gave in to their whim. He struck the ball strategically placing his banana slice into the right edge of the fairway, nearly two hundred yards from the white tees. Proud of the yardage, he backed away to allow the older coots to have their turn off the tee.

Trophy wife let out a Dallas cheerleader yell as her hubby unleashed an impressive drive, swing as smooth as velvet. Mister physically handicapped struck the ball with conviction also, both out driving Carl, balls landing safely in the middle of the fairway. Smiling, the older of the two turned to Carl, "I can not believe you're going to allow two octogenarians to out drive you, young fellow." For those of you that have never heard the term; octogenarian refers to a person between the ages of 80 and 89. Carl, speechless and humbled by the experience, could only smile and prepare for the butt whipping he was about to receive. Saint Augustine now seemed an appropriate setting for the final round. Carl had rediscovered the miracle of the Fountain of Youth in the city acclaimed for its origin. Life lessons are ageless and so were these octogenarians.

Here's Johnny

It has often been said that the vast outdoors is just a mere bathroom to the male population. Where else is this best illustrated than on the golf course. Combine beer with an average seven thousand yards of opportunities and man will prevail. God equipped the male population with the perfect irrigation system. Just like a sprinkler head, the male will shower his surroundings as if operating from a programmed timer. As men become older and as the beer consumption increases so does the frequency. Unfortunately, most golf courses strategically place only one bathroom per nine. These locations don't often coincide with the user's cycle time thus nature provides a solution. This can pose challenges when the course layout is heavily populated with homes. One of my beach buddies playing partners has devised his own plan to overcome the inadequate layout of these facilities.

Strategy can be the golfer's friend, if you know how to optimize your choices. He has devised his own to defeat the evil course designers. Azaleas are his point of focus. Not just any Azaleas, however, he will seek out those larger mature shrubs that reach heights of four to ten feet. Blooms are not required but they do enhance the experience. He'll often wave off the opportunity to pit stop at the course 'John', only to venture off on the next fairway to commune with the course's landscape or the homeowner's gardens. He treats them as equal opportunities.

We cringe as he exercises his patented maneuver. Traumatized by a zipper in his childhood, he suffers from a phobia and always unbuckles his belt and drops his pants slightly to offer up easy access to his operating system. Even though it appears he has total control, we unfortunately envision and often wager on his apparel sliding to his ankles, exposing a full moon on a sunny day. How unfortunate that would be for the entire foursome. I'm sure he'd yell "do-over" and exercise the use of a mulligan.

Mixed foursomes do cramp his style as it would do so for any of us. It's comical to observe the near panic look on his face as he now realizes he's three holes away from the next oasis. Reminds me of that commercial with the guys always rushing to the bathroom in the middle of a play or a movie, *gotta go, gotta go.* Like the road trip with the kids, "Are we there yet?" Depends would have been a better option when planning his round.

I've noticed a pattern when we play the same courses. I have a hunch that he previously marked his territory and returns to the same spot. Guess it's easy to locate, just look for the dead vegetation or recently replanted Azaleas. I'm sure the homeowners have taken soil samples or have consulted their local nursery to determine why the plants are not surviving. Azaleas are his first choice, but he will improvise if there are none available. No plant is safe.

I have another golfing friend, an elderly gentleman, who often heeds nature's call as well. I refer to him as the restroom inspector. Whether on the golf course or not, Roy will visit every 'John' at his disposal. He grades the bathrooms; bad, poor, good or excellent. When on the course, not as picky as beach buddy, he uses what's available. His club membership guarantees that he will have a pleasurable round. The grounds keeper is puzzled, why no grass will grow around that old oak on number seven.

I often wondered why they don't include urination rules on the score card. Here a few they should.

Water hazards – drop area marked (*so are the bathroom locations*)

Please do not play out of the wetlands and environmentally sensitive areas (*Do not make them wetter than they already are.*)

Natural areas are marked with blue stakes. (*It isn't natural to use these as bathrooms.*)

Out of bounds – White stakes (*urination prohibited in these areas*)

Please repair ball marks and divots (*If you must heed nature's call, please use the kitty litter provided responsibly*).

For everyone's enjoyment, please keep up with the group ahead of you. (*Limit bathroom stops.*)

Just curious, why do most men's bathrooms on the courses have no mirrors? Is it because we don't care how we look or is it because, so few men use the provided restrooms? Why have separate men's and women's accommodations? Men will use both, but women will only venture inside their own then question which woman missed the bowl or left the lid up? Let's face it. There are no "do-overs" or mulligan's when your aim is bad. You must play your first shot and we've all been prone to whiff our approach shots.

Remember, few golfers are horticulturist. They don't cultivate. They urinate. It's a man thing, not necessarily a good thing!

Rockin' Ronny

It had been almost two months since I last whacked the ball around the links. A combination of bad weekend weather patterns and other commitments had derailed my routine of at least playing once a week. I had been bowling instead, no weather delays on the alleys. Opting to use my $25 golf privileges at Wachasaw East, Little Goober Head (Eric) and I had a 12:54 Sunday afternoon tee time on a gorgeous sunny day, only a 30% chance of scattered showers. Side note: Cuz (Sammy Cannon) nick named Eric that little gem. You can't beat seventy-five-degree weather along the Grand Strand in March.

We arrived early and they sent us directly to the first tee box. We were shocked that we remained a twosome on a rather crowded day on the course. Myth dispelled, a third gent drove up in a cart stating he would be joining us. Before the formal introductions could be made, our new playing partner instigated a volley with the starter. He suffered from knee aliments and had been accustomed to blue flag preferential treatment, claim he was a member of the resort. The clip-on blue flag allows the cart occupant the right of way to drive anywhere on the course including up to greenside.

Rescue ranger said because of wet conditions this would be cart path only and no blue flags. Our new golf buddy was not happy at all and shared his frustration with the ranger, 'You must be kidding me. This is a joke, right." The ranger stuck to his guns and said, 'No joke, too wet because of all the rain we had yesterday; sorry, no blue flags.' Golfer buddy was not a happy camper. We thought he would take his balls and clubs and go back home, but an opportunity for fellowship with us must have had a powerful tug on him. Perturbed, Ronny gave in and made it a threesome.

I asked him did if he went by Ronny or Ron. He said, "You can call me anything, Ron, Ronny, whatever. They often call me Rockin' Ronny here. Someone called me that a long time ago and it stuck for some reason." Hindsight, we should have picked up on the red flag waving in our faces. Oh well. We passed on the urge to ask him how he earned that nickname. Not to worry, we would eventually learn that mystery the hard way. Each of our first tee shots landed in the middle of the fairway, so walking was inevitable with cart path only rules. Ronny's bad knees were tested early. He was pleasant enough, but it was evident that the walking back and forth to his ball in the fairway was wearing on him. Often, he would forgo it and just ask us to pick up his ball. My money was on him not making nine holes.

Ronny announced on the number seven tee box that this would be his last hole, but that was before he nailed his second shot to within ten feet of the hole for a birdie putt. He back peddled stating, "Maybe one more hole." He then missed his birdie attempt and three putted. He stuck to his guns and played the eighth and then the ninth before proclaiming, "I think I will play one more hole." Why would you make the turn and only play the tenth hole? I didn't follow the logic. Eric opted for a pit stop at the club house, so I parked and waited. Something else caught Ronny's eye on the number ten tee box. There were two more foursomes lined up behind the group we had been trailing. He wasn't too pleased and said, "They can't do that, jump ahead of us before we make the turn. I'm going to talk to the club house." Off he sped.

Minutes later I saw him approaching the tenth tee box and, even from where I was parked, I could hear him scolding the young men waiting to tee off. Eric had not returned and, with a front row seat across a small pond and seventy yards away, I watched the saga unfold. For the record, Ronny was not a big guy. I'd estimate he was about five seven, one hundred sixty pound and in his seventies. The little pit bull was on the attack. He let into the groups. "You can't jump in front of us. We are making the turn.'' Outnumbered and outgunned, eight to one odds, our new pal continued his verbal onslaught. Mister Blue Shirt, on the tee box, wasn't giving an inch and walked towards Ronny, hands in the air, doing some serious finger pointing towards him. Others from both foursomes converged. Not my fight, I had no intention of making it eight to two.

Ronny played the, 'I'm a member here card.' Mister Blue Shirt countered, 'We're all members somewhere, so what?' The discussion on proper golfing etiquette continued quite loudly. Eric returned. I quickly caught him up to speed and pointed to where Ronny was making his last stand. We agreed. We would not have his back. Neither of us were fighters and three against eight odds were still not good odds. Suddenly Ronny waved us on. Seven of the eight were hovering around him, obviously not buying his argument. I approached one lone guy sitting in a cart and informed him we didn't know this guy and had only been paired with him the last 9 holes. He smiled and said, "That's why I'm staying out of it. This is too much of an alpha male territorial dispute for me."

Finally, another guy, Mister Green Shirt tells us to go ahead. I also tell Green Shirt that we don't know this guy in case we need to make it ten to one odds against our new playing partner. Further down the first fairway we pull up alongside Ronny and I tell him, "I now see how you earned the name, Rockin' Ronny." He smiled and responded, "Did you see the huge tattooed arms on that black guy standing behind me? He could have squished me." Yes, Rockin' Ronny, I thought possibly you would have earned that whopping. I then asked him, "Are you from New Jersey or New York originally?" He says, Maryland. That's the same difference as far as I'm concerned. I asked for his phone number and house number just in case Mister Green Shirt was interested. The humor was wasted on Ronny who high tailed it to the next tee box.

To put this in perspective, Rockin' Ronny took this stance, knowing he was only going to play one more hole. Sticking to his guns and on the eleventh hole, he said farewell, saying he knew a shortcut back to the clubhouse to avoid passing by the eight behind us. We kept pace with the group in front of us, hoping Mister Green Shirt and his posse never gained ground. We had one scare though; a fast-moving thunderstorm, our 30% chance that delayed us, sending us for cover. Luckily, they must have done the same behind us. Fifteen minutes later the storm had passed. We survived to play another day, no thanks to Rock the Boat Ronny, instigator and deserter. Lesson learned. Always come to the course with a foursome and avoid making golf a contact sport.

The Wise Guy

Just anyone can't be The Starter on a golf course even though it is my dream job and the goal of many an aging Whomper. You must have knowledge of the game and that alone probably disqualifies me. My fellow whompers can testify that my play doesn't do anything to support I have a clue what I'm doing. Personality and people skills are keys because let's face it, Mr. Starter is supposed to be an extension of golf course customer service.

There's no merit in posting an open starter position because there's typically a waiting list. Bidding is probably high stakes for these positions. Some may post that they'll beat other offers by not only working for free but claiming that they would remove all goose crap from the greens and fairways every afternoon he (the lucky starter) is playing his complimentary round. Others may counter by volunteering for those 120-degree heat index days and will pull double duty morning and afternoons, again at the low, low price of zilch. After all, this is what you are getting with a loyal and dedicated starter and a senior version of *Eddy Haskell* from *Leave it to Beaver* sitcom fame, the ultimate suck-up to land the job.

Starters can be unique characters by nature. Yep I've seen a few that rate one of a kind and I'm not necessarily complimenting the person in the position. Island Green had one of these unique barkers from the shores of New Jersey. With the dialect of Tony Soprano, he subliminally articulated the pending consequences if you failed to follow his explicit instructions. Swimming with the fish might be in store for those who failed to comply with THE RULES. Or possibly becoming gator bait is more appropriate for this neck of the swamp.

My foursome knew we were in serious trouble when Mister Starter prompted us to advance to the first tee box, which in this case so happened to be #10. This required that we tee off across water, a dogleg par four to the right with a narrow tree lined fairway. Guido, our starter, asked, "*Howyoudoing?*" With a voice only the Don could appreciate. There were three groups ahead of us; translated six carts, when the Mafia-outcast yelled, "*Pull it up, PULL IT UP,*" just seconds after group number one had departed. Not that we were all that special, he yelled the same thing at the two foursomes ahead of us. He didn't tolerate any gaps between carts or groups. Fearing the consequences, we complied. Nobody wants to wake up in bed with a horse head staged for company.

Guido then instructed all but those next on the tee box to go putt. We had already putted but that didn't impact his decision for us to do it again as he pointed out, *"Youse guys got plenty of time."* Now being a true southerner but appreciating the godfather's tenacity, I immediately plunged into character doing Robert Di Nero proud, saying, *"Hey, you talking to me? I said, you talking to me. You, what you looking at?"* Well, I only spoke it loud enough for my buds to hear it. I wasn't quite ready to sign up for the witness protection program.

Guido, the designated godfather, continued, *"Fairways are narrow so keep the ball straight! No mulligans off the tee box! We got a full house and got to keep youse guys moving. If you hit the ball in the water, you can tee one up while you're standing there."* Now am I missing something in translation here? Isn't that the same as taking a mulligan? In good ole boy southern dialect I responded to my foursome, *"Whut? You ain't from around-cher is you boy?"* Even my Yankee transplanted buddy from Vermont squinted and shook his head in disbelief, stating he moved to coastal South Carolina to distance himself from this type of gent.

Speaking of, I do tire of the comments here at Myrtle Beach about the lousy southern drivers. I will be the first to admit, being born and raised in the state, this by far has the worse drivers I have ever encountered. It can bring on daily road rage and test my defensive driving skills. This is a tourist town, however, guess what? Don't let those South Carolina license plates fool you; most are not from around here! Greet one as they depart from their vehicle, *"How y'all doing"* and they will respond, *"We's doing good, howyoudoing?"*

We did finally advance from the first tee box. No one in our foursome hit into the water hazard and two of us managed to hit the narrow fairway. I, as did one of my companions, sliced to the right, finding the woods, but we were able to recover. I did par the hole and he managed a boggy. We strategically played our first tee complimentary mulligan later in the round after leaving our wise guy to greet others. *"I'm from Jersey, you from Jersey?"* But we envision the next lucky group as he barked *"Pull it up, PULL IT UP!"* If they were from Jersey, they probably understood and weren't offended.

License to Kill

Well good ole Agent 007 does hold these credentials, but I have experienced the thrill of the almost kill far too many times. Some of my whomping buddies were just not meant to be behind the wheel of a golf cart, putting in jeopardy those of us that share the cart with them. Maybe there ought to be a sanctioned driver test before one may be granted permission to drive a golf cart. As a young man, I walked with a pull cart, tough to wreck one of those. And those tour professionals just don't know what they're missing by walking or maybe they do.

Whether electrical or diesel, the ultimate all terrain vehicle can maneuver the worst contours on the course, and the drivers can overcome any obstacles placed in their path. Carts are made to go where balls go near and far. Where do I start?

Parkland Golf Course in Greenwood, S.C, a Scottish foursome format, one man and woman as playing partners, alternating shots: My female whomping buddy was driving the cart. All was well until we were completing #6, a dog leg to the left. Adult beverages had already come into play and the noon hour still lurked a couple of hours away. Maria Andretti at the wheel decided to make an evasive maneuver, without consulting her co-pilot of course. There I sat, legs extended, propped and crossed, arms folded on my chest, and a twelve-pack cooler resting on the floor between us. A hard left appeared out of no where. The cooler and I tumbled from the cart, arms, elbows, ice and beer, poetry in motion. Unharmed, but lesson learned – hold tight, secure the cooler and keep the beer away from the driver.

High Meadows Country Club in Abbeville, S.C.: I witnessed two of our playing partners back a cart down slope into a creek on #7. There was no fishing the half-submerged cart from its watery resting spot. All they could do was retrieve their bags and belongings. Big healthy boys, they huffed and puffed as they walked and carried their clubs for the last two holes on the nine-hole course. Lesson learned. Engage the parking brake before disembarking.

Quail Creek, now renamed the Hackler Course in Conway, S.C., I was almost raked from the cart by low hanging limbs due to careless driving from my cart buddy, only to then be victim of that same left turn maneuver. Fortunately, I had a hand hold and my feet were planted firmly on the floor, lesson learned and remembered.

Hickory Knob Resort in McCormick, South Carolina: I recall the *Dukes of Hazard General Lee* leap. I was the driver this time on hole #4. Let me frame the episode. Severe down slope, steep hill to be exact, and I had a good run going when we hit several deep ruts. The cooler behind the seat launched, offering up ice cube and beer projectiles, dumping the entire content on us and almost ejecting my cousin. He did manage to save the beer and most of the ice. It certainly made for interesting pop topping thereafter when his can's contents spewed like Old Faithful. It had no impact on my water bottle.

Then there's bump drafting with similar NASCAR racing results. The bumper car strategy works like this. The trailing cart bumps the leading cart inflicting whiplash to those in the lead cart; all in good fun of course. I witnessed one driver on the very first tee box, ease up and then bump one of our whomping buds lightly on the back of his legs. We laughed as he jumped. Old Dale Earnhardt thought he had his cart in reverse and pressed the gas peddle a second time. The cart slammed into buddy number two again, this time wedging him between the carts; not so funny that time. Thankfully nothing was broken during the incident.

"Rules…we don't need *no* stinking rules!" Do they really put those little wooden markers and ropes along edges of the cart paths for a reason? Apparently, we don't receive bonus points for hitting them. While playing Arrowhead Golf Course in Myrtle Beach, Bloody Carl had been my wing man for most of the round. My shot went wide right and his ball was on the left side of the fairway. I grabbed the clubs I needed and told him to bring up the cart. Seconds later I heard our other two golfing buddies yelling. I turned to see him dragging three yellow stakes and adjoined rope behind the cart. He had failed to see the marked off area. It was his 70th birthday so he was entitled to have a little fun. And I suppose cart path only usually means cart path only but that only applies if no rangers are prowling the grounds. Oh yeah, please always keep all limbs inside cart and if you don't understand this one, drive through a mud puddle while dangling a leg or while hanging your head or arms from your cart.

Bag drops are not necessarily just located in the parking lots. They can be found on the cart path, in the fairways or in the rough. Why do we tip those cart attendants if they can't properly secure our clubs on the cart? Numerous times we have lost our bags from the cart and believe me, this isn't always pretty.

Make a game out of it by trying a few of these ideas:

Drive off while your partner is either making his club selection or is trying to replace clubs.

Don't necessarily wait until your rider has both feet in the cart with butt firmly planted before you press the gas.

And never let an Obsessive-Compulsive drive because the round is all about them. They will leave you standing there with or without a club or will park in the fairway directly aligned with your next shot.

Park strategically close, partner side, to a ten-foot gator and sit firmly behind the wheel as if not paying attention.

Back up with that annoying alarm going off while your buds are striking the ball or making a key putt.

One last thing, I have this marvelous short cut maneuver I like to pull on first time, unsuspecting cart buddies. Crossing the street between holes #11 and #12 at Quail Creek, there's a narrow foot bridge over a ditch before you reach the cart path. Traveling at near full speed I veer at an almost impossible angle and caddy-corner the bridge, causing my riding partner's butt to lift into a prune pucker. I've made it so far, every time, but what might the odds be for the next time? Who's riding with me? Fore!

Incoming

On my job, before I officially retired, if I ventured from my cubicle or cubie-world as I called it, onto the manufacturing floor, I was required to wear a hard hat, long sleeves, steel toed shoes, ear plugs and safety glasses. Funny, that environment didn't seem nearly as hazardous as in my own backyard while living along the Blackmoor Golf Course. To be more specific, our house was adjacent to the #2 green, a par three hole. From the white tees to green was one hundred yards. I didn't have to buy golf balls while we lived there, so long as I wasn't picky about the brand I used. I'm a Whomper so what do you think? The bad news; there are people out there that play like I do. I warned my wife before we purchased the house. She looked at me and commented, "But you play golf, you should be thrilled living on a golf course." She didn't have a clue the dangers that lurked the fairways. Out of bounce meant we were in the crosshairs.

I rest my case. I collected over three hundred projectiles. I mean golf balls. We suffered one broken window and numerous cracked vinyl siding sections in the four-year period. We probably received hundreds of house strikes. Weekly Judy e-mailed me at work saying I should check in the yard after work claiming she had heard several direct hits. And you ask what prompted us to choose this lifestyle. I had received a job offer on the Grand Strand and we had one weekend to shop for a house. Our realtor lined up twenty-seven houses for us to view. Most were located on golf courses. I had never desired to live on a golf course as mentioned earlier. I know how poorly I play and the numerous times I've banged one off a house or condo. I'm sure I'm not a dying breed. That said, we liked this house floorplan so ends that decision.

I should have received hazardous pay while mowing the lawn, trimming the hedges and taking out the trash. Golf balls traveling at high velocity being influenced by the earth's gravitation pull make for many exciting strategic maneuvers and near misses. We've found that it wasn't even safe in our front yard as balls bounced off our roof or the neighbors landing some three hundred plus yards from the tee and a hundred yards left of the fairway and green. I should have brought my hard hat from work home.

Working in the yard became one big Easter egg hunt. I found balls in the shrubs, the grill, potted plants, lawn furniture, in the rain gutters, on the patio, back yard, front yard and side yards. I even found one lodged seven feet up in the trunk of one of our palm trees. I snapped a photo of this one before I retrieved it. Now that was a Whomper after my own heart.

When my sister-in-law, Charlotte, visited, I had to reinforce the house rules for retrieving golf balls. (1) Balls must be in our yard. You can not race the golfers from the tee box to the green and snatch up their balls that are legally in play. (2) Same applies for balls landing in the neighbors' yards. Exception to this rule is if you know the neighbors are not at home or if the balls are close enough to our yard that you can covertly pick them up or kick them into our yard. (3) You do not have to wait for the balls to stop rolling before retrieving. Once the tee shot has broken the imaginary out of boundary line, it is fair game. (4) It is permissible to hold the ball up with your left hand and wave at the golfers with your right hand, providing you display the *'it's mine"* smirk before they arrive at the green. (5) All balls retrieved are property of the house.

Speaking of Easter eggs, I began using egg crates for my bounty. I sorted them by brand name and replenished my golf bag by dumping a dirty dozen in the side pocket. When I did hit an errant shot, which was often, using this recycled variety had its perks. When my fellow Whompers helped me search for my ball and they located a ball first, they asked me what I had hit. I replied, "What kind of ball did you find and whose initials are on it?" I was covered for every response because I used every brand made and someone's initials or special markings were on every ball. My bud yelled, "This one is an Intec with the initials *AB*." I first responded, "Do I have a shot? And if the response was yes, I then replied, "Yeah, that was the last one I pulled from my bag."

While living there, I never nailed my house or even hit one in the yard. Another southern buddy and I were paired with a couple of northerners playing the home course. We stood on the tee box of the home hole and I warned the strangers not to hit in the yard left of the green. The guy was a real jerk but have no fear, I'd retrieve their ball after the round. One finally caught on and asked, "You live there, don't you?" My buddy busted a gut laughing.

We eventually moved from the Blackmoor location seeking refuge from the meteorite showers. We made a conscious decision to never reside on another golf course. Downside, I had to eventually purchase more golf balls after I used up my supply.

The Swiss Army Machete

Well I had never experienced golf in another country until my wife and I and four other couples booked one of those all-inclusive island vacations. Our destination was Punta Cana, Dominican Republic, with a package than included three rounds of complimentary golf. Four of the five men in the group were golfers. We brought our clubs with us to try island golf. I purchased one of those armored plane-resistant golf bags carrying cases for my clubs and hoped the clubs arrived when I did. I didn't anticipate the challenges of hauling the carrier and our luggage through airports. Luckily, we along with our luggage and clubs arrived safely; unlike our last trip to Vegas when our luggage arrived the next afternoon. We had nothing but the clothes on our back on that trip.

Our resort offered everything you could possibly wish for; eleven restaurants, huge pools with swim-up bars, spas for the ladies, tropical topless beaches, every imaginable water sport and equipment, and the golf course near by. Did I mention topless beaches?   We arrived on Saturday for our weeklong stay. We decided to play golf Sunday, Tuesday and Thursday. The last man standing, my brother-in-law was content to enjoy the tropical lifestyle and exotic beach. He would hold down the fort until we returned. The wives did not participate in the clothes optional venue. My brother-in-law did sport the topless option, but it lost something in translation.

We scheduled our first tee time and arrived at the hotel lobby promptly before 8 AM to await our shuttle bus. Greeted by the all inclusive 'Hola', we boarded the shuttle. Oddly, curtains were pulled on the windows. We soon discovered why. While our ride took less than ten minutes outside the resort, we traveled through third world conditions. It made us feel a little guilty about our luxuries, but we soon suppressed these thoughts once we saw the immaculate course. And did I mention they have topless beaches and swim-up bars in the pools in this little paradise of ours? The course was not topless.

We received the royal treatment and soon were off to the first tee. We had the course to ourselves with October being the off season for tourists. Painted coconuts served as tee box markers. After exchanging cameras and staging photo opts, we whacked our first shots. We couldn't help but notice that everyone at the course and grounds sported a machete. I must admit, visions of one of those hacker movies flashed through my mind; *Friday 13th, Jason Goes Topless in Punta!* Trailer: *Unsuspecting tourists get sliced and diced while whomping and whiffing their way in tropical paradise. Distracted by toned and tanned topless honeys frolicking along the pearly white sandy beaches; one by one, the foursome is faced with machete toting menaces.*

Mesmerized, we observed locals and their uncanny ability to optimize their all-in-one tool. It was no mere chopping tool for clearing a path for a safari as we had seen in the Tarzan movies. We expected to see them chopping limbs. We were taken back though by such expertise, and at the pace of a snail, how they were edging the cart paths, flower beds and curbing. Did the island have no weed eaters or other trimming tools? It even served as a digging tool, a hoe for weeding inside the natural areas and flower beds. It was an art form indeed, awesome to watch. These gentlemen made it appear effortless. I wondered if they were being paid hourly wages. Laid back doesn't even begin to describe their work demeanor.

While we didn't witness it, I'm convinced they probably shaved with it as well when not gutting fish and other animals. I think I saw a bartender cutting lime and crushing ice with his, then stirring our beverages with its tip. I could only imagine how the cards would be cut at the Blackjack table in our casino. Think I'll stick with the slot machines. We kept a leery eye on the course patrons as we maneuvered our balls over the tropical layout. Numerous attendants manicured the greenery on every fairway. They must hire them under some sort of group package or family plan. Hire one, get four more free, apparently. Each equipped with their own machete, they worked on their own assigned section of turf.

While the course was immaculate, a huge fence separated it from the surrounding countryside. John, one of my unfortunate fellow buds hooked a shot along the edge of the perimeter fence. You couldn't see through the wooden fence. As he approached his ball, a hand emerged from between some broken slates, fingering him to come closer. John glanced back at us to make sure we had his back. We smiled and nodded. He was on his own on this one. The hand withdrew and then seconds later reappeared holding three golf balls. Being a nice guy, he retrieved the balls and placed a buck in the hand. We never saw the hand again. Thing has left the course, so much for our Adam's Family flash back.

A grounds keeper approached us next riding one of those flat bed carts. Machete in hand, he pointed to a burlap bag on the cart's bed. Thoughts of heads in a duffle bag flooded my brain. He opened the bag to expose more golf balls. I feared the Thing from the fence would be offended if we bought any, so we waved him off. He mumbled something in that colorful language of theirs while giving us the look. Did I mention armed guards stood watch at every condo/home construction site that peppered these beautiful fairways? I'm talking serious automatic weapons here. I'm not sure if they intended on keeping the workers working or shooting us if we tried to escape the course. I searched for Cool Hand Luke in the work detail. How I wished I had a machete.

I should mention the heat on this island paradise. I'm talking serious sneak up on you and kick your butt heat and humidity. It later did me in. I became deathly sick by nightfall with self diagnosed sun poisoning. It took me the next couple of days to recoup from the traumatic experience. On the 18th of our first round, Mike whipped down by the heat and excessive El Presidente beers, suffered a Tin Cup moment. The road hole heading back to clubhouse had water on the left and the street on the right. Mike sent ball after ball either down the street or into the water. What inspired him to keep dropping balls until he finally landed one in the fairway is anyone's guess. It only took nine attempts. If I would have had a machete, I would have left him only holding his driver's shaft. After the round, Jerry my brother-in-law had our spot staked out on the beach. I don't recall seeing machetes thee. Then again, I wasn't looking for one.

Me at Punta Cana, Dominican Republic Course
(The only day I wore golf knickers...Too Hot...Hot...Hot!)

Cold Beer

Adult beverages and golf seem to go hand in hand, especially for the Whomping adults. I must admit, in my younger days I would partake of a couple or six cold ones during a round. I somehow convinced myself that I required a couple of beers to settle me down, so I'd play better. The scorecard didn't indicate that this strategy worked very well. Finally, I realized that it did nothing to improve my striking ability nor reduce my scores. I seldom drink anything stronger than a Gatorade now. Older and wiser I suppose.

I have discovered that the price of admission equals the entertainment value because many of my Whomper buddies do indulge themselves. This can make for an interesting round, at least for me. Their creed, it is beer-thirty somewhere rings true because they can pop a top at 7:30 AM as easily as they can reach for a cold one in the PM venue. They put a new spin on designated drivers. Most courses now prohibit personal coolers. Not to worry, most golf bags come with a built-in cooler compartment. Technology will overcome the challenges; sort of like radar and radar detectors. The system is destined to be beaten! Everyone profits. Golf = adult beverages = more beer sales = golfers making bad shots = purchasing more golf balls = more beer purchases = more rounds of golf = more beer, *you get the picture!*

I have a cousin, Sammy Cannon, aka Cuz, who can be heard yelling *"Cold Beer"* as he maneuvers down the fairways. Cuz can chugalug with the best of them. Does it impact his game better or worse? Who can say? He's having a good time and that's important to him. It doesn't impact my play so that's important to me. Consumption of too many adult beverages causes another of our buds to transform into Mike Tyson. He'll then pick fights, instigate conflicts with other foursomes, especially if they're ahead and playing too slowly or its tournament play and he thinks the other team may be cheating. This can be most embarrassing but does add entertainment value.

Why does cold beer seem to convince people they can suddenly sing? A couple of my buddies (Fred and John) after consumption of a beer or five will begin singing very strange tunes, "In heaven there ain't no beer…" One sings about coal miners doing weird stuff. Their antics seem sort of red-neckish. Both are transplanted Yankees. Yes, rednecks can come from the north. It can drive one to drink just to cope with the attempted tunes.

Wagering and beer, know that you have at least a chance of winning before you throw down the bet. Eric, a golfing greenhorn at the time, typically scoring in the three-digit range, tied John on the first nine. To put it in perspective, John wasn't having his best front nine and had shot a fifty. Eric matching that fifty felt a little frisky apparently. Cockiness is not very pretty unless you can back it up. He wagered he'd kick John's rear end on the back nine for a case of beer. How'd that go you ask? Not so good! Eric (aka Little Goober Head) didn't realize that beer was a motivator and lost the back nine by ten strokes. Beer consumption may or may not have played a factor in the original wager.

I've already mentioned being tossed from a cart along with the cooler when my not so designated driver made a radical left maneuver. I've witnessed one Whomper whiff so many consecutive times at a ball that he resembled a windmill. He responded by falling on his duff and erupting into a contagious spurt of laughter. I too have contributed to my share of ungentlemanly like behavior on the links but what happens on the course stays on the course, especially when I'm the culprit and have writer privileges. **COLD BEER, right Cuz.**

The Category One

One can never pass up free golf because there is never a bad day to Whomp the ball around the links. Three of my co-workers were graciously invited to play the Wachesaw East Golf course in Murrells Inlet by a somewhat appreciative vendor. A last-minute opportunity, this would require that we take time away from our families and any Saturday afternoon plans. We weighed our options carefully and opted to exercise Golf Kitchen Pass #15 on our wives. *Dear, we are obligated by the company to build client-supplier relations. Sometimes that means making certain sacrifices on the weekends. Look on the bright side, all expenses are covered, and it will be a feather in our hats to represent the company. Pick something you'd like to do afterwards because the remainder of day belongs to you.*

They bought it or at least pretended they had, so we prepared for our free round on a wonderful course. Life is good, belly bumps all around as we celebrated our good fortune. Little did we know that the Weather Channel had something in store for us that we'd not fully appreciate until arriving that afternoon at the course. With a windy chill in the air, we met our host in the club house. To our surprise he would not be playing with us. FFF (forced family fun) had intervened. He'd be attending his son's baseball game. He did pay in full for us and told us to have a great time. Whomper rule: Never pass up free golf, right. I felt so cheap and dirty to have taken advantage of our host like this but being a kept man wasn't as bad as I thought it would be. Little did we know that a perfect storm was brewing, and it had plans to test our fortitude and free round of golf.

The sunny weather we briefly experienced had only been a tease by Mother Nature. The winds began blowing steadily at twenty to twenty-five miles per hour with gusts easily topping forty-five. I'm sure the wind chill factor played into this on that crisp fall afternoon but our threesome without meteorological experience could only suck it up and make the best of it. We kept reminding each other that this was free golf! On the first tee we thought we were going to have to string a rope between us like mountain climbers. The wind blew so fiercely that it literally tossed us off balance. Just standing over the tee and trying to address the ball became a real challenge. It would have been a wonderful day for kite flying or wind surfing. To add insult to injury the 'Cart Path Only' rule applied due to drenching rains ahead of the cold front the night before.

It is quite amazing how the wind can redirect your ball after it is airborne. But like I said, getting it air borne had been the trick. Keeping it on the tee in the first place tested our patience. What were we doing out here we wondered. Oh yeah, free golf! Now I'm notorious for worm burning. That could play to my advantage in such extreme windy conditions. Keeping the ball low would be a good thing. For you non-whompers, worm burners are those scorching low runners that can roll quite far, instilling terror in the earth worms except for when the following conditions come into play:

(1) Water – a pond or creek will ruin a good worm burner. (2) Morning dew or wet fairways are the kiss of death. (3) Thick rough between the tee box and the short grass in the fairway will stop a worm burner dead in its tracks before it reaches the lady's tee box. As luck would have it worm burning wasn't in the cards for me that day. Hooks and slices were! I blamed those on the wind regardless of the direction it howled.

My fellow buds didn't do much better. Every shot became a battle and every fairway offered a new adventure. By the back nine, the temperature had dipped. I think we were confronting a nor'easter. Boat anchors would have come in handy. We were determined to finish our free round of golf whether we liked it or not. Still feeling cheap and dirty and now cold and wind blown, we trudged onward…free golf. I did take away some positive points. I only lost four balls and found over a dozen along the way. A good round is judged by finishing with more balls than you started. I must have had an excellent round. We might burn the scorecard afterwards.

We somehow survived what we dubbed the Category 1 on the Saffir-Simpson Hurricane Scale. We felt sure we had experienced sustained winds of 74 – 95 miles per hour. Yeah, as described under the damages section on the scale, the winds could have easily caused minimal damage to unanchored mobile homes as well as unanchored mobile golfers, damaged vegetation as we did witness airborne divots and damage to course signage. Yep, there were plenty of signs pointing to how we had blown this round. We couldn't confirm the four to five feet of storm surge but that could explain how we didn't clear some of those water hazards. At least that is our story.

We did give it a name; one only fitting since another month remained of Hurricane season. We called it Hurricane Ken in honor of our imaginary friend who rounded out our foursome. After all, our vivid imagination contributed to our version of this free round of golf. Shaking off that cheap and dirty feeling, we honored our commitment to our significant others doing whatever they had in mind for the remainder of the day, realizing that the free ride was over and that the next round would be on us.

Lightning up the Course

A beautiful but hazy southern summer afternoon, what better to do than Whomp a few golf balls after work? That's exactly what Flexible Technologies pal, Mike Bratcher and I decided to do at the Parkland golf course in Greenwood, S.C. We took the cheap route. We utilized our pull carts, opting to walk the course as it wasn't particularly crowded. The sky had that white overcast look to it, hiding the beaming sunshine somewhere above. Playing the front nine, we leisurely chased our balls from one side of the fairway to the other, bragging when we managed to keep one straight. The time period, in the 80's and neither of us was very good. Our scores were already in the forties and we still had three holes to go on the front nine, both destined to finish sixty-something.

Number seven was a slight dog leg to the right. I hooked my ball to the left and into the adjacent fairway. Mike had troubles of his own in the pines to the right, accidentally taking the shorter but more challenging route. We eventually hooked back up at the green, both of us taking double par plus two, our customary pick-up score. I thought I saw a flash but brushed it off as an eye blink because there were no dark menacing clouds or indication of rain showers. You must remember this pre-existed The Weather Channel. We had eyed the weather before leaving work. It had looked good to us.

Number eight, a par four, a long tee shot to reach a pond waiting at the bottom of a sloping fairway. If we were lucky, it only took us two shots to reach the pond about two hundred twenty or so yards away. If we were able to pull off that second lay up shot without hitting the hazard, then we had a chance at bogey or double bogey. The pond looked like it stretched on forever with the green nestled just on the other side. By some miracle we both managed to clear the water. Mike shot a seven and I managed a snowman but at least we avoided that dreaded double par plus two, ten score. Bogeys and double bogeys were pipe dreams.

Still standing on the green, I thought I saw another flash, reminding me a little like someone snapping a flash photograph. This time I didn't believe I could blame it on my eyes blinking. Mike confirmed he had seen it too. I asked him if he thought it was going to rain. He responded, "Don't worry. It's just sheet lightning. We're fine."

"Sheet lightning, what's sheet lightening?" I had never heard the term.

He clarified, "Sheet lightning is that far away flashing type, not harmful like those deadly bolts you see in the distance. We're fine. We just have one hole to play. Doesn't even feel like rain in the air to me."

It seemed like to me that it was happening more often, but I had not heard any thunder. I just figured that he must know what he was talking about. I had been taught that when I saw lightning, just count one-one hundred, two-one hundred, etc. until the thunder cracked. Each one hundred count let you know how far away the lightning was with each count equaling the distance in miles. No thunder must mean it wasn't close, supporting Mike's theory of non-threatening lightning.

We reached the number nine tee box staring at the hard-right dog leg towards the club house some four hundred plus yards away. We were almost home free. The dog leg guarded by thick trees made it almost impossible to cut unless you could command a wicked slice. Both of us being right-handers and unable to command any shot, our options were to hit the ball and see where it landed and then go hit it again. Guess what, a few raindrops began falling. The sky just didn't look like rain clouds. We both popped up our trusty umbrellas. He had honors as his seven had beaten my snowman on the previous hole. Discarding his umbrella and now being pelted by larger rain drops, he teed up his ball. I stood with my back to the woods looking a bit like Mary Poppins standing there as I spun my umbrella. He whacked his shot and in that very instance, it felt like my world had come to an unexpected end.

The so-called sheet lightning had unleashed a deadly bolt less than twenty yards behind me in the trees. In that instance, I felt the heat and whoosh of its power on my backside. My playing partner's eyes were even scarier, transfixed on what he had witnessed over my shoulder. I tossed my umbrella and grabbed my cart. He chunked his driver into is bag grabbing his cart also. Now what? Where do you go when threatened by lightning? We both realized there is no evacuation plan when you're standing in the middle of a fairway faced with 'not to worry about' sheet lightning. If you stand there with all those metal clubs, you're the tallest objects in the fairways and will be killed. You can't go for the cover of the trees because the lightning had just struck there, unless you believe it won't strike twice in the same spot. So, what do you do? Run as fast as you can to the clubhouse.

And run we did, leaving our umbrellas and pulling those carts as the clouds unleashed a gully washer and more deadly bolts. We probably should have left those pull carts and utilized a zigzag maneuver. Instead we hauled ass up the treeless fairway toward the clubhouse over three hundred yards away. We were pelted by a now hard blowing rain. Somehow, we made it with no more near missed strikes. Still rattled by the almost lightning strike and my life passing before my eyes, I looked my pal dead in the eyes and said, "Sheet lightning, nothing to worry about, just sheet lightning. I almost became the first person toasted by sheet lightning I suppose, just sheet lightning?" He said nothing.

Lesson learned, never mess with Mother Nature. Pay the extra money and ride. There is no such thing as harmless sheet lightning. Buy a new umbrella. Kick Mr. Meteorologist in the butt if he ever mentions or comments on any weather conditions. I'm just thankful to be here and able to recap the story.

Double Secret Probation

When I officially unofficially retired from Metglas in 2015 I decided to play a little more golf than I had previously been playing. I say I sort of retired and I really did, but I continued to work one week per month at Metglas helping out. Maybe it was my way of weaning off the daily grind. I did my part time gig until 2018. I had the usual bunch of guys I played golf with from work; Carl, Fred, Eric, John and Robbie to mention a few. Obviously, they weren't retired, so I couldn't count on them being able to play weekdays when I had plenty of time on my hands. Solution, I signed up for an annual golf membership at Tupelo Bay, an executive course in Surfside Beach a mere ten minutes away. I figured I could play cheap golf there when the others weren't available.

During my second round at Tupelo two gentlemen playing a hole ahead of me offered to allow me to play through or join them. I opted joining them. It beat playing alone. Martin and Ed were transplanted northerners, locals as I usually call those from the north now residing on the grand strand; more of them here than us. They thought it special as well, playing with a true southerner, one born in South Carolina. That day a friendship was born, and I became a regular playing with them. Weather permitting, they played Mondays, Wednesdays and Fridays most weeks. This was more golf than I had planned to play because most weekends I still played with my ex-working pals.

Martin and Ed had a genuine code of ethics, putting out the ball, no gimmies, even if it was a mere three-inch putt. I was accustomed to conceding ay putts within the leather of the putter but not these boys. My other pals allowed one mulligan per nine; not Martin and Ed. Every shot counted and there were no do-overs for errant shots. I abided by their rules on their turf, a running joke that Martin wouldn't allow otherwise. Now, there was no wagering and all joking aside, playing with them was very laid back with no drama to disrupt play. It was a breath of fresh air from my other playing group. Don't get more wrong, I enjoy playing with the Metglas bunch, but it could often be chaotic, one player or the other getting their nose out of joint over seemingly insignificant issues. I've been in the middle and both sides of that fence more times than I dare tally.

Over the next few months and years ahead, others would come and go within the inner sanctum of the Tupelo Boys. Martin eventually left the area and returned to his northern roots. Ed and I remained as the unofficial founding fathers. Ron, Steve, Jersey John and Marvin became regulars. Ed and I became very close friends, easily and freely discussing most any topic. Ed suffered from a series of health issues challenging him a bit, especially when the cart path only rule applied. He once shared his medical history with me; it recorded on about three sheets of paper. I think he had had about every known aliment in the medical world. I don't think I have ever known anyone who has had as many surgeries and things removed or replaced as Ed. He was indeed a walking and talking medical marvel. But, as mentioned, this sometimes compromised his ability to play the game he so loves.

When I first began playing with him and Martin, they had a couple of designated holes on the eighteen-hole course where they would take short breaks. This came to be known as the 'cracker holes'. Packs of cheese crackers were part of the ritual. Anyone behind them was waved through. It took me awhile to become accustomed to this slow play, stopping and restarting. I had never been much on patience on the course, especially taking long breaks out of the middle of nowhere. Ed, with some leg and mobility issues, might sit out several holes during the round. Eventually I became used to the cracker breaks and the much slower pace of play. I think it helped my game in the long run.

Ed, to compensate for leg issues, would often take liberty and pull close to the green to minimize the walking distance. We understood and accepted his quandary. Ed was also the official golf planner of the group. He would text us on days planned to play and what time to be at course. Another thing that took me by surprise and was difficult for me to digest was the fact that Ed never called and reserved a tee time. I had never played golf without reserving a tee time. These boys just showed up at an approximant time and expected Tupelo to work them in. This is not the way it is supposed to be. I drew on patience again and had to rethink my way of thinking. No gimme putts, no mulligans, no tee time, slow play and cracker holes…oh and Ed would practically drive on the green sometimes. It was unusual for him to get scolded by the ranger or reprimanded by a groundskeeper.

Flags are an intricate part of many sports. In NASCAR there is the green flag marking the start of the race. The yellow (caution) flag signifies a wreck has occurred and the drivers must reduce their speeds until wreckage has been cleared on the track. The favorite by far though is the checkered flag, marking the end of the race crowning a winner. Soccer has red flags indicating all sorts of penalties and kicks. I'm not a soccer fan, so I want dare making flag guesses. Red flag conditions on the beach keep beach goers out of the surf. The dreaded yellow flags on a football field can wreak holly havoc when players, coaches and fans disagree with the ref calls or missed calls. So, what do flags have to do with golf you're probably asking yourself during my latest rambling rampage?

Golf courses have flags. A flag marks the hole on the green. Different color flags indicate the hole position on the green (front, center, back). Checkered flags on the course are not indicating the winner's circle. These are warning of water hazards. Let me be clear. Warning flags do not prevent balls from going into the brink. The gentleman at the first tee sports a starter's flag on his golf cart. Roaming about many courses are rangers, a flag clearly identifying them. Rangers can be helpful but too often they are the invoker of rules, the course's version of a referee. Some rangers just can't help themselves and strive to be royal pricks, nitpicking every little thing paying customers might be doing. Slow play, too close to greens, riding in fairways clearly marked cart path only are a few of the not so friendly greetings that might be enforced.

Ed, bless his heart, hedges his bet way too often by driving too close to greens. I constantly remind him, and he interprets this as I'm afraid of the ranger. I'm just trying to fend off another potentially embarrassing moment. His reputation alone gets him in trouble. He just shrugs it off when called on the carpet. Boys will be boys and Ed will be Ed. He's lucky that rangers don't have a yellow penalty flag. He would certainly receive is fair share of 15-yarders. We finally convinced him to ask for one of those handicap flags for his cart. Having one mounted on the back of the cart does allow some leeway on the fairways. Still, good ole Eddy pushes the envelope, inching closer than closer is allowed to the greens. When it is cart path only the handicap flag is basically null and void but that doesn't stop fast Eddy during many rounds. We'll return to the clubhouse after a round and one of the guys that loads our cart will comment, 'what are we going to do with Ed or busted again I heard.' I told one of them, 'why don't you give him a ranger's flag. He's going to do what he's going to do anyway so why not legitimize his maneuvers.'

I'm fearful that sooner or later they are going to place him on double secret probation. I kidded with him after a recent round, when he was called down by a ranger for being too close to the green, that they were going to revoke his membership and ban him from the course. Undaunted, Ed again made it all about me. I was the one that was scared. As I've told the guys back at the clubhouse, don't blame me; I'm not driving the cart. At the end of the day, it's almost like a game. See who can catch him next. I guess if this is the worst thing that happens during one of our friendly rounds, it's not much to be concerned about in life's big picture.

At least he hasn't driven the cart through roped off areas like Bloody Carl did at Arrowhead. And he's not knocking over water coolers on the course like I once did at Tupelo. He's never failed to engage the brake and allowed the cart to roll backwards into a creek like my pals did once at High Meadows. He hasn't murdered a fox squirrel with a cart like I once did at Whispering Pines. There are no Ed blooper reels. Infractions are the rangers' and groundskeepers' words against Ed's, right. What happens on the course stays on the course except when I air the dirty laundry in my writing? Double secret probation doesn't seem such a big deal. For Ed, I reckon it might be like wearing a badge of honor. Everybody must be good at something. My friend, Ed Menamin has certainly found his calling.

I like how our Tupelo pal, retired ex-Ohio trooper, Marvin Jose coins it, "You lie, and I'll swear to it."

Ed Menamin and Marvin Jose

Totally Eclipsed at Tupelo Bay

How does it go? Where were you on this date when some huge event occurred? Okay then. Here goes. August 21, 2017…where were you when this historical phenomenon took the country by storm? After months of anticipation, planning and hype, the Great American Eclipse would occur on this Monday afternoon. To experience totality is supposed to be one of those 'check the box' moments.

The media circus laid claim to what was to come, Americans with telescopes, cameras and protective glasses were staking out viewing spots along a narrow corridor from Oregon to South Carolina with a rare chance to watch as the moon blotted out the midday sun to observe and photograph the historical eclipse. Supposedly those who gaze at the skies consider a full solar eclipse the grandest of cosmic spectacles. The earth, moon and sun line up perfectly to briefly turning day to night for those in the right place to experience this cosmic celestial magical moment.

Okay, the hype had obviously reached feeding frenzy proportions. As one who has embraced the world of retirement, Mondays are just another day. Well, maybe not just another day. It's a golf day, a set day, weather permitting, that I join my pals on the links for a bit of morning fellowship. Ed, Ron and Martin are usually in the fearsome foursome. Alas, Martin on this historical day in time was recovering from surgery, destined to be out of commission until October, doctor's orders. Steve tagged in to round out our foursome. Instead of our usual 10 AM tee time, Ron suggested that we should tee it up at 12:30 PM to embrace a chance at totality. Ed fired out a text to notify us of the change in plans. Cartoon symbols of various stages of an eclipse were included in his text. I inquired if anyone had those special glasses. To that Ed replied, 'No.' Ron eased my concerns with his text, 'Don't look at it.'

Let me get this straight. We were shifting our normal playing time to embrace this historical moment, and nobody had any of these silly glasses. The luster was lost for me, but Monday is a golf day so what the heck. Let me clarify. This motley crew lives in Conway, Myrtle

Beach and Surfside. None of these locations were depicted as ideal for a totality experience. Tupelo Bay Golf Course is in Surfside. To experience totality, we should be playing in Georgetown. Of course, that would require pairs of those funny looking glasses.

So, we arrive at the course and I expect to see girlish giddiness on the faces of my playing partners. After all, the premise is to play during the eclipse to experience totality, even though totality will not be experienced at our location. I still didn't get it. None of my amateur sky gazers seemed all too enthused at the expectations of striking a pick from their bucket lists. No glasses, no giddiness, nothing. Let's go play golf. During check in the attendant asks if we had glasses. She then warned us of the eeriness to expect. The daytime animals and birds would vanish as darkness approached, but the night critters would emerge. We should brace ourselves for snakes slithering into the nocturnal world. I was more concerned about the emergence of the state bird, mosquitoes, embracing the darkness and a chance to feed. Forewarned, we united as warriors, ready to do battle with woods and irons.

We pulled up to the first tee box. Something struck us as odd. Where was the starter? There was always a starter to explain the daily rules and send us on our way. Even stranger, there were no golfers in view on the course. At first, I thought Ron had reserved the course for our personal totality party. It got even creepier. The driving range was void of people whacking balls over the net and out of bounds. We were alone, the Four Horseman of the Apocalypse. Possibly I should have researched the totality of this pending episode. I feared something of epic proportions was brewing. Would the eclipse unleash vampires and zombies, with us the only defenders of chaotic circumstances? I remained on high alert.

First swing of the club and my driver connected with a monstrous drive straight down the middle. 'Eclipse, big deal, game on.' Then, it happened. My short game vanished in totality. Try as I might, it was gone. I struggled through the front nine making more pars than any of my pals. They were doubling theirs on seemingly every hole. Double pars are not what you wish to see on a scorecard with your name posted in front of them. The event was still yet to come. How could I fend off the onslaught of snakes, cooters, coyotes and alligators if I couldn't connect with my wedge? I began having visions of Lizardman, the distance from Bishopville to the beach suddenly not feeling that far.

It started innocently enough as totality approached. Mama duck and her two half grown ducklings began stalking us. Ron suggested that Ed share his crackers with the Quackers. Ed refused, now in survival mode. If an apocalyptic event lay ahead, he suggested that we conserve our food and water. I concurred; keeping a weary eye on the web-footed feathered threesome following us with evil intent in their hungry, beady little eyes. Totality would bring out the worst of the beast, so had warned the lady at the desk. Why then had she not insisted that we postpone our play? The thought entered my brain; we were tokens, mere sacrifices to ward off creature's intent on ravaging Tupelo.

Ed and Ron, Yankees. Steve and me, Southerners. North and South united for the epic battle ahead. Those wishing to defeat us would not have an easy path, this was our sworn oath. Those ducks were still there. I gripped my iron; no duffs, only ducks I silently swore. Daylight began to dwindle. The eclipse was upon us. Mondays would never be the same…that is…if we survived to see another. I glanced at my fellow combatants. They seemed unfazed. I saw no fear or dread in their eyes. I drew courage from their will to survive.

Ron received a text from his wife. Simple, 'It has started, don't look up.' Don't tell grown men not to look up, not if you don't want them to look up. Somehow, we fought off the urge to look. We braced ourselves as the daytime began to transform. Minutes passed. More minutes passed. We waited for the darkness to come, for the night critters to emerge, for the nighttime fairway lights to flicker on. Then, just like that, it was over. No darkness. No night critters. No attack of the ducks. Totality totaled to something well short of total. The eventful event was quite uneventful for us at Tupelo Bay. In a mere blink, nothing happened. At least we didn't have to fight the exodus of traffic surely to come in the aftermath. We still had seven holes to play. We had taken a few lackluster photos and selfies. The photographs looked like any other daytime pictures. Further south it was an epic event for those who had prepared and traveled the distance. Ed did use the distraction to his advantage and whipped the other three contenders in the day's round.

The next total solar eclipse in the U.S. will be in 2024. The next coast-to-coast one will not be until 2045. I just hope my short game returns before then.

Steve and Ron feeling totally eclipsed

Scuba-Duba-Do, Where Are You?

After each of us plunked our balls into the water, again, Danny says to us, "You know there are probably zillions of balls in that pond."

Rich and I had certainly contributed to that number having hardly ever cleared the water on this one hundred seventy-yard par 3. So, Danny brainstorms we could come back at night and fish them out; free balls. Playing up the pros and cons and I'm good with the con part, I tell Danny (1) there are water moccasins around here (2) we don't know how deep the water is (3) we don't know what hazards await us on the bottom and (4) it will be dark and did I mention snakes! All settled, we'll do it confirms Danny, ignoring my cons and any sign of commitment to this wild scheme from Rich or me. We were still in that twenty something age range and somewhat invincible, legends in our own minds. I must confess though; free balls did sound sort of inviting for one who at the time shot in the 130s regularly with too many lost balls. I failed to mention (5) we would be trespassing and (1) still concerned me.

We waited to a non-workday. We were employed at Flexible Technologies in Abbeville. The night of our little caper arrived. Danny went over his list. We had workable flashlights, and each had burlap bags. In the south we call them croaker sacks. Some list! I had brought snake deterrent, a pint bottle of Jim Beam. My theory drink enough of it and I would forget about the serpents lurking in the murky water. We inconspicuously parked our car on a lonely adjacent access road. Being the only car, it stood out like a sore thumb. Then using the cloak of darkness, we weaved our way across the fairways of the course until we located our objective, my nemesis, the dreaded par 3. With a full moon now appearing from behind the clouds, we didn't need the flashlights and the darkness didn't exactly cloak us as planned.

Not on our list, swim trunks, so we stripped down to our tidy whities. Mama always said to have on clean underwear because you never knew when you might be in an accident. I drew no comfort from having clean underwear in case of a snake bite. Three brave men, croaker sacks in hand, ventured into the abyss unsure of our harvesting technique. Easy enough, we could feel the balls with our bare feet. Simple, reach down and pluck them off the bottom and into the collection sacks. In deeper water this required a head dunk. Observation, a wet burlap sack with balls does not float and becomes quite heavy. Technique change, abort bags and toss balls on shore and collect them later. The water never got any deeper than our shoulders thankfully.

Soon the shores resembled the aftermath of a hailstorm. This is when the reporter says that the hail was as large as golf balls. Change in strategy, someone had to go on shore and begin collecting and bagging our booty. I volunteered and exited snake infested waters suiting me just fine. Funny thing though, water provides buoyancy and after consuming most of a pint of whisky this is a very important and pertinent detail. My legs were like rubber and my head became a spinning top. I rocked and rolled, swayed, staggered, stumbled and fell, having absolutely no balance but I had overcome my fear of snakes. Picking up balls became quite the challenge and extremely hilarious from my perspective. Neither Danny nor Rich found the humor in me whooping and laughing and giggling loudly, echoing my drunken stupor across the open expanse. Eventually they called it quits and retrieved me and the remaining balls. Croaker sacks full of golf balls and I are very heavy for those getting us off the course.

Final tally, we recovered over 1200 balls and after sorting out the shag balls, we still had over 800. Most people like me don't attempt to hit good balls across water. Probably a good percentage of those scuffed ones were mine. We set up shop selling good ones and shag ones at discount prices and had plenty for personal use. We raided several more ponds on different courses and honed our technique. I was never allowed to bring along Mister Beam again but thankfully I never saw a snake during any of our excursions.

Fast forward some thirty or so years and now living in Pawley's Island I would never consider doing what we did back then. Forget the snakes. We have gators to contend with here. I no longer drink bourbon and if I did, no amount would blur out that threat. Wiser, maybe, I'm older for sure and I do play a little better. Plus, I can afford to buy balls, but those par 3 water holes do still take a toll on my game, but, after all, it is only a game. Life is too short to approach it any other way. One side note though, we have observed scuba drivers on several coastal courses emerging from the murky ponds with plenty of golf balls. A group of my friends were playing the Blackmoor course with the number 9 hole adjacent to a watery abyss. Bubbles alerted them that something ominous, possibly a giant gator, was surfacing. Instead, the diver popped up, removed his mask and greeted them. I wasn't with them but have observed the same scene at Tupelo Bay. Scuba-duba-do!

We were before our time I suppose. What we would have given for a scuba dive outfit and tank. Second thought, Mister Beam in a submerged state might have doomed me from ever surfacing. Young, bullet proof, wild and crazy, now those were the days and I'm just glad I survived them.

Masters of the Game

For those who play the game or are learning to play the game or aspire to play the game, let me be the first to enlighten you. Everything is not included in those instructional videos, golf manuals or lessons you might choose to take. Trust me, life's experiences open many more scenarios in the gentleman's game. The impossible is possible. It's you, a tee, a stationary ball and a club. Looks simple, doesn't it? Strike the ball and it is bound to go somewhere. Oh yeah, if you don't whiff it, it most certainly will go some place. My philosophy, I hit it and if I am lucky, I will find it and will be able to hit it again. A shot leaving the tee box and going reasonably straight is considered a victory. Distance is highly overrated if you have missed the fairway, landed in a pond or lost your projectile. Here are some 'bewares' that aren't necessarily in the golfer's guide playbook.

Charting your scores, some people think this is a helpful tool. There could be much to learn by documenting your rounds, writing down scores and listing memorable events. I've tried this technique and have even utilized a spreadsheet or plotted my rounds on a trend chart. What can one learn? How can someone shoot an 89 then in a span of five months shoot a 124? I justified these actions by reminding myself that I merely re-qualified my WGA (Whomper Golf Association) card. Furthermore, being a quality assurance professional, I convinced myself that it was perfectly acceptable to remove outliers from the scoring to ensure the statistics were sound. I tossed the 124 but exercised quality privilege by keeping the 89.

Research, reading and videos can be helpful if you can apply discipline, mind over matter and utilize the principles and practices theory. Carl is a student and visionary. He reads the do's and don'ts from golfing magazines and then mentally prepares for the game and attempts practicing what he has learned. Does it work? Maybe not all the time but mentally preparing for the game can't hurt I suppose. If all else fails, he always has an ample supply of mulligans to ensure the endgame, the score card reflects positive results. Mind and matter, if it doesn't matter what you really shot then say you shot something better. Stuff like this ensures that you return for another round.

Cold Beer, now some think the correct number of adult beverages can improve the game. Consumption of too many might convince you that you are playing well and having fun, but your playing partners might have a different perspective of the results. Beer consumption has its challenges. Most courses will not allow coolers. Strategy prevails. Stash beer in your bag. Sneak to the parking lot at the turn and replenish. Or, make the cart girl a happy girl, buying those costly beverages every time she passes. It is never too early to indulge for those who apply this strategy. Flasks are an alternative to storing a twelve pack in the golf bag.

Home on the Range, many opt to perfect their striking ability on the driving range. I learn nothing from the driving range. I like many, fear I am wasting good shots there or I'm hitting so many bad shots it will impair my thinking when we begin the round. Negative vibes before the round can never help. Plus, I tend to try to hit the basket of balls as quickly as I can. I'm a man possessed with empting that basket of balls as quickly as possible; can't help it. Thus, I learn nothing. I do have one friend that prefers range play. I call this *Technique by Eddie Belcher*. It goes like this. Simulate 9 holes on the range rotating club selection for par 3, 4 and 5 hole set-ups. Putting may be a problem. Then tally up your score at the end. If you can shoot a 65 (for 9) on the range, then surely you can replicate this scoring on the links. Killing them on the range at plus 200 yards then killing them on the course same distance but in the woods doesn't translate well though. Lesson: Fairways are not as wide as ranges. Why don't they locate houses, condos, women and children, highways or ponds on ranges? It would better simulate actual playing conditions. Plus, there aren't any nets on most fairways.

The Perfect Club doesn't exist for the Whomper. My Three Club Rule: Pick something to get you off the tee, something to hit in the fairway and then something to get you in short from the green. Keep all those other clubs in the bag for show. Over the years my technique has changed. In the early days I played irons (a 1, 2 or 3),

189

even off the tee box. I couldn't hit anything that had a big hunk of wood on the end of the shaft. To be honest, my irons weren't that good either but were the lesser of evils. Now I use a driver, a seven wood, a 13 and 15 wood, and an assortment of wedges. Some refer to my technique as Old Man golf. Hey, I'm old and resemble it now. I'm always on the hunt for that perfect club. My clubs all have extreme loft like 14 degrees for my driver and 38 degrees plus for fairway clubs. I'm a sucker for the $1 and $2 consignment variety. Expensive clubs don't improve my game. I go cheap.

Back pain and golf are common bed partners for many. Professional golfers often travel with a chiropractor, especially if they are prone to back woes. I can't count the times my back has locked up on the course, sometimes in mid swing. What to do when it happens? I just hope I can survive the round, riding and sitting out the play. Sometimes it is painful sitting, standing or walking. Carl refers to his as seizing up during the round. One good thing about having Carl along is that he usually has an assortment of medication in his golf bag, pain pills or muscle-relaxers. I call him *Doctor Feelgood* and rely on his diagnosis and prescription to assist me when necessary. My other playing partners usually won't offer up a friendly massage. Good friends are hard to find.

Being the minority on the course is not something I signed up for. Possibly, minority is the incorrect analogy. More appropriately might be anomaly. This perception was never a problem when I resided and played golf in the upstate of South Carolina. Since 2005 we have lived at Myrtle Beach though. The tourist community is far removed from my hometown in Abbeville. Some visitors have told me that they have never met a real local, saying I'm their first. Locals here are from New York, New Jersey, Ohio and Canada. Most of my playing partners are foreigners; I mean northerners.

Throwing club tips: Break it before tossing it. Throw it in the water. Keep a few 'yard sale' clubs in your bag and replace the offending club with one of these and toss it. Never break your putter unless you have a spare. Throw a partner's club. Ask this question to partner first "Do you think you can whip my butt?" If the answer is yes, without a doubt; then rethink tossing a club from his bag. By now, the mood has probably passed any way. Never throw a club you need or that cost premium bucks.

Driving the cart on Par 3 fairways: Pretend stupidity. Have an obvious limp or better still, a cane or walker. Point to your cart buddy and begin cursing when the ranger shows up. Make sure you have a way back out. I saw a couple do this then had to back track all the way to the tee box with next group waiting to hit. It wasn't pretty. Refrain from driving onto the green or through sand traps. Move the cart signs as you go. Tell the ranger it's your first time to play golf and maybe he'll let you off with a lesser warning.

Slow play is slow play. Brother-in-law and son-in-law in same cart, same course, same green, same world; slow play, get it. Thumper and Cuz in deep conversation as if they haven't seen each other in decades; slow play will happen. The OC boys lining up a putt; leave them on the green and go to next tee box. Grandkids don't know any better. Lead by example. Forget golf etiquette, furthest away hits first; play hurry up golf and hit the ball if no one is in your line of fire. Should we really let that twosome play through? Pay close attention to their antics behind you before making that call.

It's okay to hit things providing you take the appropriate penalty. House, condos, vehicles, pools are usually out of bounds. Hit another ball and take the penalty. Hitting the forward tee marker, a fellow golfer or golfer in another fairway might prompt a do-over from your playing partners. Pinecones, rocks, roots, move them or your ball if not in tournament play or if you don't have a wager involved. Utilize root rule to move your ball to your best advantage. Flower beds and shrubbery might be considered a free drop if they are not located well out of bounds in someone's yard. If you are unclear on a free drop, look for any sign of windmills or dinosaurs; just saying.

Inconsiderate homeowners might come into play. Lawnmowers, leaf blowers and weed whackers, the curse or the deaf homeowner, a do-over might be justified. Barking dogs, screaming children, hammering on construction sites, utilize these interruptions to your favor.

Out of bounds is out of bounds. Yell fore before the ball lands and strikes something or someone. Shout from the tee box for all women and children to go inside until after you pass. If you retrieve your ball, always yell to your golf buddy that you found theirs. If your ball hits anyone, accept that it has and point to your playing partner. Unfortunately, golf courses are not designated hard hat zones. Know the stats for golf course deaths? Are you more likely to be struck by lightning, hit a deer with your auto, bitten by a shark, run over by a truck, attacked by killer bees or hit by a golf ball? Another good practice is to never look the homeowner in the eyes if your shot goes wrong. Keep driving or walking and pretend that wasn't your shot. If they call you out, pretend to not hear them. If they persist, fall and fake a stroke or heart attack.

No Tress Passing signs apply only if you get caught. Try standing in front of the sign and trick your golf buddy into retrieving your ball. If he gets caught you can openly scold him in front of the homeowner. If these tactics bother you, then ask for permission to enter the yard or just leave your ball there. Remember, always practice the honor system when you see that bucket of balls and sign "3 for a buck" in the backyard. Now we know golfers are not honest so why would you use the honor system? Worse case scenario, those who pretend to leave a buck and take half dozen or just dump the bucket in their bag and hightail it.

If you have an OC player in your group, try to be understanding and helpful. Never rearrange their clubs in the bag. Don't switch club head covers. Refrain from scratching through scores on card to make corrections or scribble them in poorly. Not a good practice to pile all your empty cans and trash in the basket behind cart seat on top of their club head covers. Unzipping their bag pockets might not be the best policy. Pull off and don't give them a chance to arrange their clubs at your own risk. Make sure you always drive the cart. Often, they do enjoy being in charge. It can be quite stressful if you point out a spot on their clothing, on the back of their shirt or seat of their pants, somewhere they can't verify. Walking or standing briefly in their putting line might unhinge them. Reminding them how wet and muddy it is and then point to their clothes again might handicap their game. Coughing and then accidentally taking a swig from their beverage container is never the best practice, nor is never allowing them to finish a sentence or a story. Whatever you do, never mention that you noticed something strange or different about their stance, back swing or grip. Be considerate as much as possible.

Lessons from the golf professional: Lessons should be taken when you're young enough to appreciate them and while your mind can sponge in the training. I bet the pro never told you some practical approaches on the course like telling you to purchase a ball retriever. Trust me when I say this; size does matter. Retrieves come in extendable ranges from six to eighteen feet. Choose the eighteen-footer because they will retract to the length of a common driver. This can not only come in handy when you've hit your ball in a water hazard. It can be useful for retrieving your ball from briar patches, poison ivy and near alligators. It's my version of the universal club. No, you can always see the bottom eighteen feet from the bank, but you might be surprised how often the eighteen-footer comes in handy. When not fishing for your ball, you might be retrieving your friends. If play allows, you might fish your limit if you find the ideal location where balls appear to be spawning in the water. Keep retrieving until the group behind you catches up or until your playing partners wear thin on patience. Offer them some of your bounty to fend off their displeasure.

Curse of the Good Shot: Bloody Carl owns this one. I always cringe when he proclaims good shot while my ball is still in flight or roll. Almost one hundred percent of the time this little innocent comment guarantees that my shot is not going to end up in a happy place. If he says, nice or good shot, my ball usually rolls into the trap, the water, out of bounds, in the woods or lips the hole. You're going to like this one dooms me to some hellish outcome. Worse, you didn't see where the ball went and neither did they, but they claim it sounded like a good shot. Or we lost it after it hit that second tree. Cart buddies are sometimes too often occupied within their own universe to be part of yours. Or they forgot to tell you about that water hazard or bunker until after you have found them.

The Tupelo Boys…Jersey John, Marvelous Marvin and I have ten-foot putts for pars on number 8. Jersey John standing over his putt, says, 'I'm contemplating.' Marvin lining up his putt, says, 'I'm concentrating.' I add while eyeballing mine, 'I'm constipating.' All three of us nail our par putts, the power of the 'Cs'.

Being the master of the game is not for the weak. Such is the game of golf. Sometimes it isn't that masterful either.

Oh yeah, this is a little disclaimer. If you have noticed I sometimes repeat the same stories or situations. just pretend to ignore them. It's my version of a mulligan and sometimes they are endless. Just a reminder, these were written over a period of many years and old people, like me, forget I have already told them.

There's No Place Like Gnome

I have often mentioned that I don't do golf wagers. I recognize a losing bet and the Vegas odds on me losing. There's nothing wrong with offering a reward for best in show on the course. This concept gradually evolved while playing with a select few of beach buddies, coworkers at Metglas in Conway. Jamie, Greg. Eric (aka Little Goober Head) and I were the founding fathers of this unique trophy play. After all, if there is a friendly competition then a winner deserves first place, and losers do not qualify for a participation reward. That's not the way it was ever intended to be. There are winners and there are losers. It makes you stronger and competitive. Entitlement paves the road for whiners and complainers. Work, win and reap the benefits. Golf, yes, it is but a game, but it is a competitive game, you against the course and yourself. And, if the format is agreed upon, your score against your fellow golfers, even if no money is involved.

I digress. In high school, my junior and senior summers, I cleared right-of-ways for Abbeville's Little River Electric Co-op. During our midday lunch breaks we often played a card game called smut. The loser each day had the curse of carrying home the 'smut belt.' This was a mythical belt, supposedly meant to be the lineman's belt. Said to be a curse because owning it was supposed to bring you bad luck. The winner and other participants won nothing but were just happy not to wear the smut belt. You never, and I mean absolutely never, wanted to lose the last hand on Friday. That destined you to carrying the belt over the weekend. Nobody wanted to contend with potentially bad luck until Monday. I mention this little toss back memory because friendly competition came into play, no money exchanged hands.

Think about it today. College sports often involve rewarding standouts with some sort of belt, like those awarded winners in championships from the wrestling and boxing world. Some colleges have huge linked chains with large significant medallions recognizing a potential game changing defensive or offensive play by a player. I bowled and won my fair share of bowling trophies. I never won one for last place or for merely showing up. But that smut belt was indeed the ultimate loser's recognition. Still, all for fun, you couldn't help but wonder if it brought bad luck. I'll say this; if you had it and anything bad happened, it made you wonder. It presented a subliminal heavy burden for those dreading to take it home. Okay, enough of the mythical and cursed smut belt.

Golf among friends deserved to be something special, something recognizable and off the chart. I've racked my mind but can't recall how we decided on our trademark trophy. But it was always up for grabs in every round we had at least two participants playing. It didn't matter if the current holder was one of those playing. If he didn't play, it was understood that he forfeited his opportunity to retain it by not being present. The treasured trophy was a six-inch-high Gnome. The Gnome represented everything. The lowest score won it and would proudly flaunt it on their desk at work until the next round. There were no handicaps and no strokes given. It was a straight up win, scores versus scores, two, three or four players. Rules were simple. One mulligan was allowed per round, taken when claimed on any shot, including a putt. Once used, it was gone. No endless variety in the Gnome game. Briefly, we did have a fifth participant, Bloody Carl; but after the first outing, he realized that he no longer had a front nine and back nine mulligan, only the one. And, there wasn't the usual endless variety he was accustomed to using. Root and rock rules were allowed but no improved lies from repositioning to advance your next shot. He gracefully bowed out of the competition and played his game, his scoring options. No heartburn from the rest of us, we were solid at four.

The Gnome exchanges hands often, ownership proudly displayed. Jamie was the best of the four of us. Winning the Gnome usually required him playing poorly and one of us having an exceptional game. The Gnome was a red hat wearing garden variety purchased by me at a consignment store for a couple of bucks. There wasn't anything special about it, but the Gnome was all powerful to us that vied to cherish and flaunt it. Coworkers who had heard of the legend would ask us after we played, 'Who has the Gnome now?' The Gnome represented the ultimate accomplishment among friends. All was fair and fun in a round of golf, if approved by your fellow competitors. The animated feature, *Gnomeo and Juliet* debuted in theaters during the reign of the Gnome. I've even written a book, *The Tenth Elemental*, which involves a Gnome named Jimmy. I haven't published it yet.

Sadly, the battle for the Gnome came to an abrupt ending. No, we didn't break or lose it. No, the competitive spirit didn't die. Sometimes there just is no place like Gnome. Jamie, our fiercest competitor, and his wife, Kim who also worked with us, had decided to move back to their home territory in Pittsburg. It just seemed to be appropriate to have one final game for ownership of our precious prize. I don't remember who possessed it at the time, but we decided to put it up for grabs one last time. The winner would be a forever winner and holder of the Gnome. The Tradition golf course in Pawley's Island had been selected as the final battle ground. No, the course held no significance in the grand scheme of things. It just had cheap rates at the time. Cheap golf was a major contributor in the world of Gnome. Our regulars, me, Eric, Greg and of course, Jamie would be doing battle to possess the iconic cornerstone in our game. Pictures are worth a thousand words and happy endings or meant to be, especially among wonderful friends.

And the prestigious Gnome goes to…

Jamie receives the coveted Gnome from me for final round win at the Tradition Course.

Me, Jamie and Eric (Little Goober Head)

Rope-a-Dope, *Float like a Butterfly, Sting like a Bee*

We've made many memories at the Arrowhead Golf Course in Myrtle Beach, some good, some not so good. The layout includes three 9-hole courses, Lakes, Waterway and Cypress. Lakes and Waterway, by name, sound more treacherous than Cypress, don't they? Any course that includes something watery in its name usually suggests hazardous wet challenges to those hoping to shoot a descent score. Yes, while both courses have their fair share of water potentially coming into play, it is the dreaded Cypress course that can quickly insult your integrity and ability to have a great round. The first four holes especially will make or break you. The four holes from hell are what I call them. Trust me when I say there are other holes on the course that are just as challenging and forbidding but those first four are round breakers if played poorly. You never know which two courses you are designated to play until the starter tells you. Average or sub-average golfers stand breathless, hopeful that Cypress will not be on the menu.

I'm one of those who pray silently that Cypress isn't the starting or finishing nine. Funny I should feel this way. My best score and the only time I ever broke 90, happened on the Cypress- Lakes combo. It's 2019 now. My record round happened December of 2007. I shot 44-45, 89. Finishing on Cypress is never how you'd like to end your round though. I suppose that's better than starting on Cypress. Then again, stranger things can happen. Destiny can hide in the bushes and spring out and surprise you when you least expect it. This is a plot twist warning; more to come, just keep reading.

Arrowhead is where we hooked up with that Southern Belle, the cigar smoking club pro who wowed us with her something well below par play. We finished that round wishing we could play like a girl. I for one never achieved that level of play and never will. Arrowhead also has a special local perk. Play four rounds (tracked with playing card) and get the fifth round free. Plus, they do give locals a discount rate (drivers license required) while tourist pay primo bucks to enjoin the southern ambiance.

I should have clarified this earlier about Carl, aka Bloody Carl. I call him Bloody Carl because since he battled cancer a second time and underwent aggressive chemo, he now bleeds freely almost at the mere touch of his skin, had invited us to his birthday celebration. He would be turning 70 that fateful Friday and golf was his birthday gift to himself, courtesy of a kitchen pass from his beloved Maryanne. Carl embraced the Bloody Carl nickname, claiming Viking heritage. Arrowhead was his preferred golf course for the outing. A round of great golf was his birthday wish bequeathed for himself. There's absolutely nothing wrong with having worthwhile expectations. Raising the bar and goal setting is thought provoking. Executing might or might not be problematic. The birthday boy would control his own destiny, maybe.

Rounding out the birthday foursome would be two co-workers, Mister Extreme OC, Fred as mentioned in previous chapters. The fourth would be a first timer with the group, Ronnie from human resources. Ronnie had no idea what he had signed up for but, now committed, he would have to judge the outing for himself. My three playing partners were already sampling adult beverages before the morning round began. I held the designated position; designated for what might be anyone's guess. I'd chauffer the birthday boy and be the official score keeper, something I could do on a golf course. Driving a cart is much easier than driving a ball. Well, for most people it is. The birthday boy was excited and ready to begin his ageless round on a gorgeous Myrtle Beach day. The starter greeted us and announced the two courses we would be playing, Cypress and then Waterway. The birthday party would be starting on Cypress, say it ain't' so.

So, we began on Hole #1 of the first four from Satan's watery abyss. I double bogeyed as did my cart buddy, Bloody Carl. Next up, one of the toughest Par 5s I have ever played, hell hole #2, a long winding left dogleg, fairway feeding downhill right to left. I came just shy of meeting and greeting the neighbors in the houses on the right. Bloody Carl was short but down the middle. I hate this hole and a have doubled pared more times than I care to remember. A double bogey is a major victory for me. I launched a decent seven-wood from the upslope side of my good neighbors residing just below. It ended much better than I could have hoped, giving me options. Pitch a layup further down the fairway for a shorter crisscross water shot or live dangerously and go for the green protected by a much wider water crossing. Carl played the safe layup. I usually screw up layup shots, so I pulled out my trusty 13-wood, the distance further than I liked, but what the heck. I made it, hit the green and over a hill behind it. I had never been across this water in three shots. Carl hit his next one in the water and finally skipped his sixth shot across. It was Carl's birthday, but living the moment, I made a fifty-foot chip off the hill and into the hole for a birdie. I had never pared this hole, much less experienced the perfect miracle.

I double bogeyed the next one, a 145 yard Par 3 across the water and then pared the next Par 4 across the water, completing the four holes from hell with double bogey-birdie-double bogey-par. I was ready to flip a cartwheel but it was just a mere notion, wiser and older now. Carl was struggling and had lost balls on three of the first four holes; not what the birthday boy had envisioned. We somehow survived the deadly Cypress. I had three pars and the birdie for a 46 and thought about another cartwheel. Visualizing a flawless one is better than executing a failed flip flop. Not to worry, things were heating up for the second nine. Carl had not fared well on his first birthday nine, too may balls going places that they shouldn't. Onward to Waterway, the worst behind us, right?

I was still playing above my pay grade while Bloody Carl wasn't having the best of birthday rounds. The fourth fairway is a straight away Par 4 with the picturesque Intracoastal Waterway flowing to the left. My second shot was on the right near the green. Carl was to the left, so I asked him to bring up the cart. I'd take what clubs I needed and walk. Halfway there, I heard our other two companions yelling Carl's name. I turned to see birthday boy dragging three stakes and the attached yellow rope behind the cart. He had failed to notice the staked off ground as he drove toward the cart path and had driven right through the ropes. Resourceful, he screeched to a stop and then began replacing what he had just ripped up. Later he would claim that he had being breathing in the scenery and had not seen the stakes and rope. He had the cart on the ropes though, doing the rope a dope his way. This would be a birthday to remember, one that he wouldn't forget, nor would we. I guess that's why it was worth telling again.

A few holes later we would experience another one of life's little blooper moments. Everyone was on the green. I had just putted out and was heading to retrieve the cart. I again heard my golf buddies yelling Carl's name. My first thought, no cart, no ropes so what now? I turned to see that Carl had fallen backwards and was rolling on the green, no tuck and roll technique engaged. After we made sure he had not injured himself, the razzing began. He claimed his rubber cleat had snagged the green and had caused him to fall backwards. He hadn't floated like a butterfly, but I bet it stung like a bee, both physically and emotionally. I'm surprised no one said, 'I've fallen and can't get up.' But, we didn't; maybe out of respect for the seventy-year-old. I was just glad he had broken nothing but maybe his spirit.

We ended the round with no more Ringling Brother's rope tricks or acrobatics. We should have blamed everything on Ken, but we forgot to invite him. Wayne wasn't along either to buy the beer. What good are imaginary friends if you don't utilize them for special occasions? Bloody Carl certainly provided us with a memorable 70th. I ended up shooting my second lowest round, 46-46 for a 92 and on Cypress once again. We reminded him that this was his birthday month, so we had at least three more weeks of celebration, more rounds to play to commemorate his. Good ideas sometimes go bad. We played another round the next week at Arrowhead. My luck ran out on Cypress. Carl rode with Mister OC this time. Two obsessive compulsive players in the same cart is always a recipe for disaster. We had memories, none like before. Not to worry, we'd have one last try for birthday month.

We needed a change of venue and opted to play River Oaks. The OC boys rode together once again, Carl driving. He officially dubbed the ride the Crazy Train. River Oaks also has three nine-hole courses, The Fox, The Otter and The Bear. The starter said we would be playing the Fox-Otter. The endless mulligan would come into play as would plenty of psychotic behavior on the Crazy Train. I pointed out all the roped off areas to Carl, some were bonus rounds, five stakes and ropes, just in case he wanted to go for the record. He managed to stay clear of them. Guess he didn't want bonus points. On the Fox's seventh hole, Mister Tumbling Tumble Weed reared his ugly head once again. Midway to the green on a long sweeping Par 5, the amazing tumbler once again lost his footing and fell backwards. He came away unscathed again, but we feared he was pushing his luck. One of these times he was going to break something. He said he needed to start wearing shoes with no cleats. We certainly couldn't argue that point. In two days, his birthday month would expire, thank goodness. The OC boys survived another round in the same cart and so did we, happy to have both eggs in one carton. For the record, I broke a 100 again, my pre-birthday wishes met, hoping I would have a good birthday month come May; no ropes or tumbles hopefully.

All Aboard the Crazy Train

Golf is not a game for the thin skinned or those with oversensitive emotions. Golf buddies can offer the best relationships, but they can also ditch out their fair share of cruel and sarcastic comments. There's the serious golfer, business like, no kidding around, playing by the book in search of the perfect game. No. That's not me. As I have pointed out numerous times, I can't play with serious golfers. I'd ruin the round for them and me too. Choose wisely when you pick your playing partners. Even the vetting process isn't foolproof. Incompatibles often sneak through and pose a more challenging dilemma like how to cull them from the herd. I'm sure some of mine have contemplated how to tactfully cull me from playing the game not meant for me. Quirkiness and idiosyncrasies are only tolerable when you're as equally quirky and out there. Welcome to the Crazy Train as Carl has framed those square pegs struggling to fit in the round holes while often testing our very last nerve. And yes, possibly adult beverages enhance the craziness or tranquilize those dealing with it.

What qualifies one to be a passenger boarding and then riding the Crazy Train? Shall we explore the possibilities? You must remember. Golf for me has covered a time span of nearly forty-five years. The Crazy Train has always existed even though in namesake it only surfaced recently, not long before I decided to publish these short shots. Instead of approaching this from the beginning, let's start now (2019) and work our way backwards. After all, moving to the beach community and now in the golden age of my life, retirement, I play more golf now than I ever have. More golf doesn't necessarily equate to quality golf, but heck, any golf is good golf given the alternative. It's mid-June and I've already played over sixty rounds this year. Enough said about that. All aboard, the Crazy Train is departing the station for golf courses along the South Carolina Grand Strand.

Game day might be on any course in the Myrtle Beach area. We're all about playing cheaply and seeking the discount rates. Location really has nothing to do with the behavior of those sharing your golf cart or paired in the other cart. The crazies are just that. Sometimes the round appears to be normal other than the friendly barbs being tossed about on the first tee box or before the round begins. This is expected among those I am accustomed to playing with. I am just as good at it as my playing partners are. This is normal for us, not the Crazy Train version. As the round progresses, you'll know quickly if the Crazy Train has pulled into the golf depot. It might surface when one or more pals begin crooning wild and often off-color songs. There is no assigned seating for the politically correct or incorrect. Duets from the Crazy Train are not destined to make America's top forty. Adult beverages are usually in play and consumption of mass quantities enhances the process, not necessarily the ability to carry a tune.

Those commuting on the Crazy Train can become hypersensitive. Something as simple as walking in their putting line can set them off like a firecracker. On and on and on, there is no end to their relentless reminders, replaying the incident as if it just cost them the Fed Ex championship. Praising one golfer for making an incredible shot while not recognizing Crazy Train's shot is taboo on the course. Crazy Train will point out quickly, 'what about my shot?' It's all about me has never been spoken louder. Shouting and whooping might happen at any moment and for no obvious reason. Yes. Adult beverages apparently do improve one's ability to vocalize loudly. This might irritate your playing partners or any golfers within five holes of where the call of the wild happened. Restrooms can sub as recording studios, the echo affect upping the ante for those belting out the silliness while relieving themselves.

You have decisions when dealing with the Crazy Train passengers. Ignore them. Call them out. Refuse to play with them. Quit playing golf. Forgive and forget. To each his own how one faces one's demons. Choose wisely though. Friendships could be on the line. Is a silly game and is equally outrageous behavior worth losing a friend over? Let's continue. No need jumping needlessly and regretting it lately.

Those riding the Crazy Train have one track minds when the beverage cart approaches. Golf isn't the only game in town when beer is to be had and had and had some more. Those who have not purchased a ticket for the train might find it disturbing and quite disruptive while standing over the ball preparing to hit their shot. The occupants of the Crazy Train are oblivious to anything beyond their immediate world. And, believe it, the world belongs to them. More beer, more banter and more loud behavior, seemingly beer instills deafness to those consuming mass quantities. Forgetting it is their time to hit the ball isn't unusual behavior. Forgetting to shush while you are trying to hit the ball becomes more the normal. I'm not shy about pointing this out to them. Do-overs are commonplace for some.

Everything becomes important and eventful from the Crazy Train's perspective. Conversations become magnified, especially when a playing partner is addressing their ball on the tee or in the fairway. Telling a joke or sharing an opinion is the equivalent of the runaway train. Nothing is more urgent than what is on their immediate mind and on the tip of their tongue. You have choices yet again. Step away from your ball and wait. Step away from your ball and give them that Medusa look. You know the one I'm talking about. Your wife uses it flawlessly all the time. Maybe clear your throat and toss up your hands. Or just call them out, "Hey, I'm trying to hit. Do you mind?" It is okay to throw your best hissy fit if you think it will return things to law and order. It might even make you feel better too.

The singing has finally wound down. Maybe they've exhausted their song selections, or the adult beverage tally has quenched more than just their thirst. Not to worry, there's no such thing as catching a break from the Crazy Train antics. You now hear music. It doesn't take long to zero in on its origin. It is coming from the Crazy Train cart. Cell phones sub as radios unfortunately. Any song can be accessed with the help of Google or a play list. I'm sorry. Music doesn't belong on the golf course during the round, singing or playing kind. Save it for your shower or car. Crazy Train knows no shame. Everything is humorous or pertinent, videos included on those same smart phones. I always turn down the volume or mute mine before the round. That doesn't occur to those riding on the

Crazy Train. Tools of the trade are as important as the clubs in the bag.

There's nothing worse than some passengers on the Crazy Train experiencing a bad round. If they are playing bad, they are taking someone down with them. Misery enjoys company at the bottom of the heap. More loud behavior can be expected to disrupt other players. Whining and complaining reaches new volumes. Choices again, fall for the trap or do your best to ignore the ploy. Confrontations can go ugly quickly. When I'm in the middle of a tailspin I try my best to not disrupt my playing partners' rounds. I'm the one having the bad round, not them. Sometimes I try to walk it off. It doesn't always work though. I bite my tongue and try to climb out of the deep hole I've dug, in most cases the round already ruined for me. If I don't there will be another round hopefully. I'm a Whomper, remember. Terrible golf is a gift, but not one for giving and spreading to those you play with frequently.

I must confess though. I have had my moments and one shameful one comes to mind, my ticket punched for a trip on the Crazy Train. Eric (Little Goober Head) and I were playing the Parkland course at Legends in Myrtle Beach. Clarification if I failed to do so; Sammy Cannon (Cuz) came up with the name 'Little Goober Head' for Eric. It means nothing more than calling someone you 'Little Smart Butt' or other affectionate names. I digress; back to my shameful event. When keeping score, instead of writing down the exact number of strokes for each hole we jot down how many strokes we are over par. Example, a bogey would be recorded as a 1, a double bogey as a 2, etc. It makes it easier to total at the end of the round how many strokes over par we are. I had scored a 1, then a 2, a 3 and a 4 for double par on a par four hole. Eric commented that if I had a double par on the next hole, a par 5, I would have a natural straight on the scorecard. He laughed saying he would have to keep the scorecard if I did. I was getting progressively worse and didn't find any humor in his sarcastic remark.

Subliminal thoughts planted, how would the par 5 play out? I hit a terrible tee shot, short, straight up in the air. I worm burned the next setting me up for a long attempt over the environmentally unfriendly swampy area. Next shot, you got it, I whomped into the swamp. With the penalty I'm now hitting my fifth shot and I'm over 200 yards from the green still. Fifth shot doesn't clear the swamp either. I'm dropping six hitting seven and it lands in the crap too. I'm pissed having allowed the dreaded double par thoughts to infiltrate my head. I toss my seven-wood into the air and behind me. Tossing a club is something I never do. It goes backwards over my right shoulder. I turn to see it heading toward Eric and the cart thirty yards behind me. The seven-wood catches the cart's window frame on the driver's side where Eric is sitting and snaps into, both pieces lodging in the frame in a V-shape. My moment of weakness could have ended in tragedy, killing my playing partner. I humbly asked his forgiveness then tossed both sections of my go to club into the deep woods, disgusted and embarrassed. What was I thinking? I could have gotten the club head re-shafted. Life on the Crazy Train isn't pretty. I punched my ticket that day.

Enough of now golf, let us digress further. The Crazy Train travels other tracks and carries many other passengers. Craziness is always defined by the level of crazy disruptive to the rest of the foursome. The so-called Crazy Train can also be associated with actions, those that are singular to the person performing them and not necessarily an act that might cause others to play poorly. Here are a few of my favorite examples. A new coworker shows up at the designated morning tee time at Blackmoor golf course in Murrells Inlet, rounding out our foursome. None of us have ever played with him, a new guy at our company. Single, he admits he had been out all Friday night. He's obviously feeling no pain from his nightly activities. On the first tee box he pulls out a fifth of bourbon and another fifth of vodka, asking if anyone needed a drink. We pass but he mixes him one, more alcohol than mix. For the record he's not being loud and obnoxious, more subdued instead. We are in observation mode for our early morning round. Soon he is addressing his ball, teetering forward then back on his heels, attempting to zero in on a nonmoving ball. It isn't working. Before we complete the first nine, poor guy is out of it, sitting motionless in the cart. We needed a bungee cord to secure him in place. I don't think he remembered joining us. Point taken, he was eventually terminated at work because he reported to work snookered and passed out at his desk. He left shortly thereafter and never remembered being there.

Let's pursue the art of club tossing. Not mine. Mine was a onetime lesson learned event. Another Eric (not Little Goober Head) in our Wednesday Whomper's group hits his wedge over the 8th green into the woods at the Cedar Springs course in Greenwood, S.C. Frustrated by his approach shot he follows this up by tossing his club in the same direction, a helicopter blade twirl technique. Now his club is lost along with his ball. Reluctantly he goes in after them. He does locate his club. Cedar Springs, Everett this time, after a bad shot, pounds his club on the ground snapping the head off the shaft. Same guy, same round, miss hits ball from woods and aggravated, wraps that club around a tree. It's funny how we golfers blame bad shots and rounds on our clubs. These are the same clubs responsible for good rounds and shots. Same buddy completes a substandard round at Persimmon Hill in Saluda during our annual Flexible Technologies tournament. When the rest of us completed our round, he is sitting in his car waiting for us, all four doors open and trunk popped, racing his car engine. He fishtailed out of the parking lot, not willing to hang around for the trophy ceremony. I think that's last time we rode with him on the Crazy Train. Jerry, another coworker and same tournament, tossed his golf bag into one of the lakes after the tournament. He blamed them for his disappointing round. Bad clubs shouldn't have misbehaved. Poor golf bag though, a causality of golf war. That would show them. These weren't a cheap set of clubs nor was the bag.

Crazy drivers should never be allowed behind the wheel of a golf cart. Some must drive mopeds based on the way they drive carts, no license required. Be careful when you're the one signing the golf cart waiver and then allowing your cart buddy behind the wheel. You remember me making that mistake and allowing Bloody Carl to bring the cart up to the green at Arrowhead. He took out those stakes and section of ropes marking where you weren't supposed to drive on the course. Flexible working buddies Pat and Charlie exited their cart at High Meadows, neither setting the parking brake. The cart rolled backwards into a creek. No number of people could restore it to dry ground. We tried. Crazy Train people don't always think things through. I've been thrown from carts, the hard left doing me in along with the cooler. Dukes of Hazards jumps can send the contents of a cart flying. I've taken out a course water cooler and stand at Tupelo Bay by not gauging my attempt to turn around. They now secure that water cooler to a pine tree because of people like me. I set a poor example for My Cheap Gold date on that round. No. There were no adult beverages involved, just a poorly executed maneuver.

Tupelo Bay in Surfside Beach, one of our playing partners temper sometimes gets the best of him. He confronted a twosome behind us because they had almost hit into us a couple of times. I thought he and the female of the twosome were going to go at it. She wasn't taking anything off him, and he wasn't given an inch on his perception of their play. I'm not sure who would have taken the best out of three falls in this one. This isn't the first time our pal has been involved in a confrontation on this course. He had developed quite the reputation, well known even by the course staff. Unjustifiably so, he and another playing partner got into it because the playing partner thought he was starting a similar argument with another group behind us. This time our pal was completely innocent. His reputation haunted him though, escalating the situation. Sometimes you can't catch a break riding the Crazy Train.

Yep, the Crazy Train has room for an assortment of characters. I've seen my fair share of wild and wooly events, situations bizarre and behavior unruly. Even the best of buddies can get their nose out of joint for insignificant reasons. After all, we are all human, right. Friendly disagreements or button pushing moments can and will occur when least expected. The key is to forgive and forget. That's not so easy for some folks. Egos and personalities tend to clash when big kids play games. I've had my share of misunderstandings and disagreements to last me a lifetime. That was the old me though. The new and improved version, old and now retired, has mellowed. I really try hard to not allow situations to get under my skin. Life is too short. I do my best to be the peace maker-golf therapist. Sometimes I get through to those agitated at others. Sometimes I don't. One thing for sure, I will not take sides when adults act like kids. I'm tempted sometimes to make them go pick out a switch and give them what they deserve. It's okay to occasionally beat your kids to let them know you love them, even if they ride the Crazy Train.

The OC boys as the Witch

Kirk, Jerry and Me at Possum Trot

Snowbirds and Seagulls

Snowbirds & Seagulls

SEAGULLS &
SNOWBIRDS &
FIRST UNITED METHODIST

A Senior Adult Ministry

of

First United Methodist Church

901 North Kings Highway

Myrtle Beach, SC

Phone # 843-448-7164

Email: office@fumcmb.org

Website: www.fumcmb.org

2019

Snowbirds are typically retirees who wish to avoid the snow and cold temperatures of northern winter but maintain ties with family and friends by staying there the rest of the year. Many migrate to the Grand Strand for up to four months during the winter. Our church,

First United Methodist, located directly across from what was once the Myrtle Beach Pavilion parking garage, established a welcome program for these travelers years ago. It begins in January and is aptly titled Snowbirds and Seagulls. We, those living here fulltime, are the Seagulls. The Snowbirds are welcomed and encouraged to participate in church and church programs. Seven weeks of Tuesday golf outings are scheduled, providing discount prices at different courses playing under the captain's choice format. Thursdays from January through March are meals and entertainment for the visitors and participating locals.

I participated in this program as a seagull in 2019 for the first time after I retired fulltime. It provided an excellent opportunity to meet the visitors, to spend time with church members and play golf. I'll be the first to admit that I'm not an advocate of the captain's choice format. It's just not my cup of *'tee'*, everyone playing a shot off the tee and then all players playing from the best shot location. I usually play my worst golf. It's something about playing my own ball that keeps me engaged in the game. Sometimes my worst golf shows its ugly self then too. But this is meant to promote fellowship. There are no awards or trophies. A winning team simply wins and everyone else doesn't. I tried to embrace the concept and accept it for what it was meant to be. As it turned out, I really enjoyed it and even finished on a winning team once out of seven outings. It was an extremely cold day with eleven people (three teams) showing up. Worst our threesome could have finished was third. We somehow beat the other two foursomes. I've attempted to capture some of the more memorable moments as follows:

I missed the first outing at Pine Lakes in Myrtle Beach but was able to join them on the second outing at the Tradition in Pawleys Island. I showed up but they didn't have me listed as a participant. I was a man without a team; what a way to begin my inaugural round. Not to worry, Big Tom our retired pastor saw to things. I was seated with Big Tom and Rick, another church member, in the bar and grill area, and mentioned the dilemma. Big Tom stepped away for a moment and then returned saying he had added me to his and Rick's team. A snowbird, Roger, from Kentucky would be our fourth. We old guys, under 75, would play from the forward tees, the ones I usually play.

Anyone 75 or older but under 90, would play from the lady's tee. Two would play from that tee box. Anyone 90 or over would play from a tee box in front of the ladies. Big Tom qualified giving us a definite equalizer.

Play began. I could have sat in the cart on most tee boxes. My best drive was insignificant with three other members of group hitting from forward tees. My play in general was very pathetic, curse of my playing this format. Big Tom finally told me to make the putts. Directly after his instructions, I sunk a downhill sidewinder twelve-footer for a bird. Always listen to your elders. Rick gave me a bit of friendly critiquing on my fairway shots. He said I made good contact but my 'towards' was off. In other words, I was hitting the ball in the wrong directions most of the time; not helpful to the team concept for sure. We managed to survive the round with an under par score but nowhere close to those finishing first or second. After the round, Big Tom told everyone that no team had more fun than ours, saying he laughed the entire day and enjoyed it more than any previously played round of golf.

Big Tom commented on how he considered himself blessed to have excellent health for a man in his 90's. He felt for those elderly folks that have so many health issues. He continued, saying he walked 10,000 steps each day and tried to go to the gym four times weekly for workouts. He said, thankfully, he took only one pill each day for his thyroid. He laughed, saying the pill is so tiny, that if he drops it, he can't find it. Big Tom also collected contributions from the golfers, snowbirds and seagulls for a charity he supports; feeding children in three surrounding counties. One dollar would feed ten children. Big Tom and his son, Tommy, a local attorney, would both match every dollar contributed. He eventually collected and they matched funds to feed over 7000 children. He would later joke when taking a collection during one of the Thursday programs that Tommy didn't know he was taking this last offering. Not to worry, he said he would drop by his son's office and tell the financial secretary to make out a check to the charity. Big Tom is a natural magnet for donations and fund raisers. Although I had known Big Tom for years, he and I developed a wonderful personal relationship during the Snowbirds and Seagulls program.

I met another Tom (Tom Marsh) during this program from the state of West Virginia. He and I became instant friends and I invited him numerous times to play golf with me and my local friends during his three month stay. He had been intrigued by my knickers wear and asked where I had purchased my attire. The next time I saw him, Laura, his wife told me that they had gone by the Knickers Store and Tom had picked out a pair. She said they were going to have to make him a pair because they didn't carry tent sized. Cruel, even for one's beloved but they both laughed about it, clearing the way for me to laugh too. If I close my eyes and listen to Tom talk, he reminds me a little of Larry the Cable Guy. I realized how close our friendship had developed when Tom, while eating some Oreos during the round, asked me if he had any in the corners of his mouth. I pretended to wet my fingers with my tongue and clean it for him. Many months later I had an opportunity to play golf with Tom in Princeton, West Virginia on the Pipestem Course. Tom told me then that he now carried a mirror in his golf bag so he could check for Oreo crumbs. I said, "Not a compact." He nodded to confirm I had guessed correctly. My back was ailing during my visit there and Tom had taken a fall the night before we played, tripping over a table, launching his glass of milk and dish of pie into the room. He handed me a Motrin that morning before we started our round and took one too.

While at the beach, I had been telling Tom that he and Laura just needed to move Myrtle Beach so that we could play golf year-round. During a round of play his beloved phoned him. Before ending the call, he handed the phone to me. I pleaded my case to Laura, telling her we'd find them an ocean front home. She quickly told me that Tom could move to the beach tomorrow and that she'd miss him. After the call I looked over at Tom and said, "Boy that was easier than I thought. It's okay for you to move." One last Tom tale; on Valentine's Tom asked me if Judy and I had any place we went for this special occasion. I said, "Yeah, home. We had outgrown the desire to participate in the hustle and bustle." Tom nodded, telling me that he and Laura usually picked out cards together and read them to each other. Afterwards they put them back in the rack.

217

Then there was Snowbird, David. During a round with him and two others at Wild Wing Golf Course, it was cart path only. Captain's choice not being my format as mentioned, I designated myself as the official retriever of drives that we weren't going to use. Further into the round David tried to take my job, overreached and stepped on my profession. Finally, I agreed to take him in under my wing and began teaching the grasshopper the protocol of being a ball-go-getter. He's still on probation but is coming along. I attempted to point him to a greater calling, to be the flagpole holder on the green. Stubborn, he had his mind set on being the ball-go-getter, so I allowed him to follow his dream. At the next Snowbird-Seagulls program he brought a couple of balls tucked away in his pocket. He tossed them across the floor to test me. Backfired though, I prompted him to retrieve them and demonstrate his technique. I decided to keep him on probation a bit longer.

Dan, a local, Steve, his Snowbird friend, and John, another snowbird were paired with me. The weather was cold and blustery. All of us were bundled up for the round at Whispering Pines. Steve, a New Yorker, wore short sleeves. He said it was sub degree weather back home with plenty of snow. This weather was more like paradise in comparison. I had a running joke with Dan. Every time he had a bad noncontributing shot, I put him in the penalty box until he could redeem himself. He occupied the box regularly. He thought muttering a few 'Hail Mary's' would absolve and free him; not on my watch, my rules. Tom Marsh and his group finished seven under par, the winning team when we played Wild Wing. The last outing at Litchfield Country Club I was grouped with Tom Marsh, Ron and David (still on probation). We matched that seven-record breaking score with a seven of our own; seven over par. We could not make a putt inside of four feet. I told Tom he was the other one who could claim being part of a fourteen-stroke swing. Scott was behind us that day and couldn't believe how many balls we hit into the water. He said to me, "Tell me that wasn't your best tee shot I witnessed you guys playing from the woods." I nodded my head saying that personified our round. I also bragged about the time I got my first swimming pool on a course. I played on three teams with Roger from Kentucky. He claimed he had never been able to pay enough money to keep me off his team. Roger also carried this cute pink butterfly net for retrieving balls from his cart.

In all the silliness I've covered, one cannot deny the wonderful fellowship we experienced, Snowbirds and Seagulls bonding and becoming lasting friends. If anyone took the game seriously, they didn't allow it to impact the outings. This was only a seven-week league. I hated to see it come to an end and eventually see our new friends head back north. There's always next year. West Virginians Tom and Laura had already confirmed their reservations for next year's three month stay. It will be a long hot summer before they return, and we can do it once again. But as previously mentioned, we did venture to West Virginia many months later where I played that round with Tom before two bus loads of us headed to Baltimore to catch a cruise ship for a nine-day trip up the east coast. Laura arranged the trip.

Shoeless Joe Jackson

Time for a little history lesson that has nothing to do with golf but does play into the theme of this short shot. Joseph Jefferson Jackson played baseball in the early 1900s. He is best remembered for playing with the Chicago White Sox in the 1919 World Series in which his teammates participated in a conspiracy to fix the series. Jackson, because of his association with the White Sox and what was named the Black Sox Scandal, was banned from playing baseball after 1920 by baseball's first Major League commissioner. Jackson had led both teams in several statistical categories, set a World Series record with 12 base hits. Still, his association with teammates accused of throwing the series, cost him his career while still in his prime. After the White Sox lost the 1919 World Series to the Cincinnati Reds, Jackson and seven other White Sox players were accused of accepting $5,000 (equivalent to $72,412.14 in 2018 United States Dollars) each to throw the Series. In September 1920, a grand jury was convened to investigate the allegations. Jackson played for three Major League teams during his 12-year career prior to the scandal.

According to Jackson, he got his nickname during a mill game played in Greenville, South Carolina. Jackson had blisters on his feet from a new pair of cleats, which hurt so much that he took his shoes off before he was at bat. As play continued, a heckling fan noticed Jackson running to third base in his socks, and shouted, "You shoeless son of a gun, you!" and the resulting nickname "Shoeless Joe" stuck with him throughout the remainder of his life. Lesson complete, so you're obviously scratching hour head and wondering what in the world does this have to do with a golfing tale. Allow me to expand on the title's concept. Shoeless just seemed too appropriate for the following golf bloopers.

Sammy Cannon, my cousin (aka Cuz, my brother), was cursed with forgetfulness. Some of my most enjoyable rounds of golf were with him. All I have now are those precious memories. He lost his battle with leukemia in 2018 at the tender age of 67. I miss him every day. I'll mention it now and probably several more times before all is done. I published a tribute keepsake book about Sammy titled *Cuz, My Brother, Life is Good, God is Good*. It is my favorite book hands down. And I didn't make a penny on it. It was sold at cost for those like me that loved the man. Okay, back to the Shoeless Joe theme. It became a running joke between Cuz and me that I verbally go through a checklist before leaving for a golf game. The list forever grew as it became painfully obvious that other items must be added. I'd ask before we left, 'Cuz, do you have your visor, your glove, golf balls, golf Garmen, sunglasses, regular glasses, etc.' But wait, it gets better, much better. He and his bride, Judy, visited us regularly at the beach. We would always plan golf outings if possible.

We were getting ready to head out and Cuz asked could her if he borrow a visor. He had forgotten to bring his. Once he forgot to bring ankle socks to wear with his shorts (typical beach golfing attire). Another time he didn't bring enough golf balls. On another occasion we were scheduled to play a round at Myrtle Beach National with Little Goober Head and Bloody Carl. Upon arrival, Cuz realized that he had not brought his golf shoes. Bloody Carl allowed him to borrow his tennis shoes that were close enough to Cuz's size. That at least got him out of his dress loafers. The kicker came on another occasion when arrived for a weekend stay while the girls were slated to go to Charleston for a weekend Christian conference. He had forgotten to bring his golf bag and shoes. How do you plan a weekend of golf and not bring the tools of the trade? That was Cuz. I scrounged up some clubs; had an extra bag but we still had to venture out for him to buy golf shoes, glove, balls, tees, etc. Shoeless Sam Cannon, I rest my case. Oh yeah, I had to add his temporary tooth to the list while he was waiting for his permanent partial.

Raymond Sanders, my brother-in-law could drive you batty when the game of golf was involved. He and my son-in-law were the two procrastinators featured in the short shot, *La-La Land*. He and brother-in-law, Jerry, were batching it with me one weekend while the four sisters were away having their girly weekend. I had to work the first day of their arrival at the beach. We lived adjacent to Blackmoor's par 3 second hole. Upon my arrival, around 4:30 that afternoon, Jerry is in the sunroom and low and behold, Raymond is

221

on the green putting. I yell to him that he can't be doing that while rounds are still in play. He promptly tells me that he's been getting off the green when golfers are on the tee box. I'm obviously furious and tell him to come inside. He does, still wearing his cleated shoes, which I promptly tell him to remove. Undaunted by my anger, he nonchalantly removes his golf shoes and heads to his bedroom. Later he returns and we begin discussing our dinner plans. Jerry comments to Raymond, nice shoes, that he has a pair like them. As we plan to leave, Jerry goes to his bedroom and comes back claiming he can't find his Reeboks. Yep, you guessed it; they are his feet. We have a good laugh but find it peculiar, his behavior.

Raymond is a diabetic and it's in October. We had extra Halloween candy left. My Judy tells the boys to help themselves to it. Jerry later discovers the trash can in the bathroom filled with candy wrappers. Good ole diabetic Raymond in one day has consumed most of what had been enough candy to feed four for the weekend. We didn't at the time suspect that Raymond was in the early stages of Alzheimer's. During a later visit, Raymond and Brenda, Judy's sister visited us for a short stay. Raymond kept complaining to her that his shoes were too tight. Brenda ignored him. After they departed days later for home, Judy discovered that one of her best pairs of Sketchers was missing. You guessed it. Shoeless Judy had lost them to Raymond, the disease taking its toll.

Raymond Sanders with Me

Not all shoe episodes include kinfolk. I mentioned Tom Marsh, my
new best friend from West Virginia, in the previous short. Tom and
two of my ex-coworkers have just completed a round at Sunset
Beach's Sandpiper Bay in North Carolina. I had picked up Tom at
North Myrtle Beach on the way. I had lifted the back-hatch door and
begun removing my golf stuff from the golf cart. I paused to
converse with the other two gents parked close by, recapping the
scores and discussing the fun day of play. I then removed my golf
shoes and reached for my street ones. They were nowhere to be
found. Had I left the car unlocked and had I become victim of a shoe
thief? Of all things, why would anyone steal my shoes? This had
never happened to me. Frustrated I verbalized my discontent.
Laughter behind me disrupted my verbal assault. Tom pointed to his
feet. He was wearing my shoes. He commented that they felt a tad
too tight. Get this. I wear size 101/2 and he wears size 12. Tom had
not brought a change of shoes and had worn his golf shoes. He
claimed mine looked just like his. Mystery solved, I felt much better
and we'd get a lot of mileage from this episode. Upon retuning to his
condo and as he placed his golf bag in his SUV, he showed me his
pair of black shoes, exactly like mine, apparently larger though. We
shared a second belly laugh. Some of the craziest things happen on

the course. Sometimes whatever happens stays there; other times they are just too bizarre and fun not to share.

Tom Winn and Tom Marsh

If My Papa John Bowie Would Have Played Golf

John Bowie, my Papa, born in 1900, passed away at the ripe old age of ninety. That seems like yesterday to me, his only grandson. Never a golfer, his pastimes were hunting and fishing. During my childhood he always took me to both. I have tried to visualize what a round of golf would have been like if I had talked him into joining me. The corners of my mouth immediately go north just thinking about it. No doubt, it would have been a hoot.

First, I'd certainly have to pay because he'd never fork over the price for admission if a day of fishing wasn't included. He always fished free or visited his favorite 'dollar a day fishing hole.' Next, I'd have to find a course without dress code restrictions. He'd most certainly be wearing his Camel brand denim overalls. Picture this, a two hundred pound barrel-chested, bald and toothless southern grand old man joining me wearing my Par 4 knickers for an afternoon of playing the gentleman's game. Now wouldn't we have been a sight in the fairway, or the way I hit the ball, in the woods, which would suit Papa just fine.

Standing on the first tee box, looking over the lush green fairway, I can hear his first comments, "Son, that there would sure make a good garden spot." He always had these huge vegetable gardens and would figure fairways were just a waste of good farmland. He might add, "You could raise a goat or two out there."

I'd probably tee up the ball for him and hand him my driver. He'd be wearing a pair of those cotton work gloves on both hands. He'd hand the club back to me, reach down and pick up the ball and then pull out that hand crafted sling shot from his overalls, his weapon of choice when hunting rabbits. He'd load up the ball and fire that puppy. The ball would land out there in the middle of the fairway about a hundred fifty yards off the tee. I'd then suggest, "Maybe you should get back in the cart and just ride, Papa, and enjoy the scenery." I'd be green with envy that he placed his ball in the middle and farther than my shot.

Squirrels scurry left and right across the fairways. I then notice that scary little twinkle in his eyes. I place my hand on his hand, still clutching the sling shot giving him the look of disapproval. On the Carolina Grand Strand courses huge grey or black fox squirrels typically hop right up to your cart, standing on their hind legs as they look for a quick handout. Never turn your back on them or leave food in the cart because they'll steal it. I can hear Papa say, "Lookey yonder, Hon, at the meat on them bones. These critters are a lot bigger than the little grey ones I usually nail back home. Heck, I could snatch him up and put him in the game basket behind the seat of this little car we're riding in."

I. again, reinforce that the golf course would not appreciate it if we began slaughtering the local wildlife. He tosses them one of his goobers. That's boiled peanuts for you that don't understand the goober term. I notice he still has that stew pot gaze, so I speed off to our next shot. Yep, taking him on an outing in Myrtle Beach would have been memorable indeed. Visualizing, I can imagine Papa staying easily entertained as we continued our little trek through the wild kingdom. On number five, three turkeys cross the fairway, all gobblers, and I have now taken possession of the sling shot for good. I am warning Papa not to throw any golf balls. Doves flutter by and he encourages me to try to nail them with my seven-wood. He asked, "How much do they charge you if you just want to hunt on this parcel of land?"

I spot the course ranger approaching. I quickly convince Papa that he's a game warden and I then tell him that we're on game management land. He tips his hat as Mister Ranger rides past us. He behaves for a while, but I'm not ready to drop my guard just yet. I boomerang a hook into the pines to the left of the fairway. We ride over to search for my ball. I avoid saying let's go hunt for my ball, fearful I might get him started again. The pines are thin. Thankfully I find it quickly, turn and see Papa with my driver in his hands. Only bad thoughts come to mind. He's staring up a small hardwood, club cocked like a deranged baseball player in a denim uniform. He's motioning me to join him; not good.

He tells me, "Walk around the other side of this here tree." He's now applying his patented treeing technique to a fox squirrel perched head high on the opposite side of the tree. One person stays put while the other one walks around the tree. The squirrels will circle back to the opposite side providing a clear shot. Respectful of my elder, I tactfully remove the club from his grasp and then I lead him back to the cart. I ask him politely not to try to kill anything. He shrugs while giving me a curious look.

We somehow make the turn with no fairway trophies. I buy Papa a coke, salted peanuts and a hotdog. He pours the peanuts in his bottle of coke sloshing them around and frequently taking a swig. Because he left his store-bought teeth at home, he pulls out his pocketknife and carves the hotdog into tiny bite sizes that he can gum down. I dread the back nine because several ponds await us. I have this special gift for finding the water with my ball. That will take us too close to a potential fishing hole.

I'm now standing on the number ten tee box, overlooking an ominous pond. I've suggested that Papa remain in the cart. As predicted, he has eyed it and says, "Hon, take out the rods; we done found us a fishing hole! Hit another one of your worm burners and scare us up some red wrigglers. It's about time we wet our hooks and drown a few worms." I do my best to ignore his request and then I slice my drive, where else, in the pond. I drive over to drop and play my third. As we pull away, he yells, "If you drive really slow, I could troll from this little car." He has my ball retriever in his hands scooping at the water. Pointing to the beverage cup holders he tells me that we could put the bait worms in them. He then spots the cooters sunning on the bank and I must hold him in the cart to keep him from going grappling. Grappling is when you wade in the water and reach under the bank trying to find catfish and snapping turtles.

Finally, we're heading down the eighteenth fairway. I've had to talk him out of grappling in two more ponds. Pulling up to the club house, he greets every group asking them what they got and how many. Interpreted this means did they catch any fish or kill any critters, and how many. Golfers interpreted this as the old dude wanting to know how many birdies or pars they had and their final score. I didn't try to intervene and just allowed the conversation to fall where it fell. Taking Papa golfing; what was I thinking? And boy am I lucky that I never did. It would have been something though.

Papa and Me
(I had just landed my first fish by myself with a cane pole, a five-pound catfish)

Our version of Me and Mini-me!

Oh yeah, that accidental homicide that I committed at Whispering Pines would have taken on a slightly different twist. Papa would have claimed that belly up fox squirrel for supper. It would have been like feasting on a Thanksgiving turkey.

The Immortal

My dad, Thomas Jefferson Winn, stricken with Parkinson and Alzheimer's much too young. It soon halted his weekly golf, no longer possessing the motor skills or mental capacity to play the game he loved. He and I took up the game at different times in life and having conflicting schedules, we had very few opportunities to play a round together. I can probably count on one hand how many times we did.

He never played the game during my years as a young man still living in the household. I flew the nest at eighteen and didn't play my first round until the ripe old age of twenty. I sucked and never took the game seriously. Over the years I played the game in spurts, often playing no more than three or four times a year. I didn't start playing with any regularity until I leaped into my forties, then playing our Wednesday Whomper afternoons. I still sucked but had fun with those that shared my same skills. Later we would relocate to Myrtle Beach where I began playing golf almost weekly. That would be years from now. I'll stick to a before time when my dad still walked this earth.

Daddy didn't take up the game until after his early retirement from the textile mill, after forty some odd years of working for the same company, Milliken in Abbeville, S.C. In his late fifties, he decided to begin playing with three of his cronies a couple of times a week at the nine- hole High Meadows Country Club. This is the same place where I whacked my first ball. I think one of them gave him a used bag and set of clubs. He enjoyed his time spent with them. I worked days and they played mornings, so tee times seldom worked out for us to play together. The first time I did play with him, I realized like father like son, he sucked too. I guess the whacker doesn't fall too far from the fairway or in our case one must first find the fairway.

I recall a story about him playing a round with his nephew, Bob, and friends, deciding to hit his next shot. The foursome putting out on the green ahead were in no danger of his short distance worm burners, a shot I also mastered. Guess I inherited it honestly. You guessed it. He nailed one, hitting one of the unsuspecting golfers in the leg. Dad, not necessarily known for his strategy on the links, quickly handed Bob Winn his club and walked toward the cart. Bob had been left holding the bag or club in this case. He waved and begged forgiveness and lucky for them, the victim accepted the unfortunate great shot as accidental. I never did ask what dad shot on that hole.

As his health declined, he eventually reluctantly walked away from the game. His buddies really hated it as did I because we never had the chance to do some serious golfing together. A young man in his sixties, a silent heart attack struck him first, followed by Parkinson with a twist of Alzheimer's thrown in just to seal his fate. Cruel diseases they are; one punishes the body while the other steals your mind. He had lived a relatively healthy life until these unforeseen diseases transformed his world to one of uncertainty.

During a family gathering one Sunday afternoon at our home in Greenwood, the guys decided to play Par 3 West, a neighborhood nine-hole par three course, all five playing from my bag. I brought dad along thinking it would be good for him. He still had some motor skills but rarely articulated more than a one or two word sentence. He lacked the ability to make conversation. His face had lost all expression, almost zombie like. I'd catch myself wondering what he might be thinking or if he was even capable of provocative thought. I felt I had lost him already.

On the first tee box, I regretted my decision to bring him along. I teed up his ball for him, gave him a nine iron, but sadly he couldn't comprehend which direction to hit the ball. My heart ached when I watched as he addressed the ball in the opposite direction of the green. Each hole thereafter I aligned and positioned him for every shot. His shuffle walk became increasingly challenged by the contour of the course. Another bad on my part, I hadn't considered his inability to walk the course. There were no carts. This would most certainly be the last round we would play together. I would sadly remember this one for all the wrong reasons, so it seemed. I agonized watching him hole after hole knowing he shouldn't be there, but we tried to push on and complete the nine-hole round. He did make contact most of the time once I positioned him in front of the tee and got quickly out of his way. Robotic is the best I can explain it, each swing appeared so mechanical and rigid, his face void of all expression.

We were now on the sixth hole, one hundred thirty yards from tee to green. I did as I had been doing on every tee box. I clutched his shoulders and then strategically aimed him toward the green. His shot worm-burned thirty yards off the tee. I guided him to his ball and realigned him for the next shot. He struck that same nine iron, holing the rounds only bird from a hundred yards. The six of us started whooping and hollering, not believing what we had just witnessed. We began patting him on the back and telling him what a great shot. The joy on his face was priceless. He laughed and I really believe he understood the feat he had just pulled off. Regrets, extinguished. We could have quit then because I had just experienced my best round of golf.

Soon after, he became bedridden. He fought this curse for over five years. He outlived each of his golf cronies, several brothers and sisters and even my mother, his caregiver, who died of pancreatic cancer three months after being diagnosed. Dad passed away three months after my mom, a tough thing to experience for an only child, but for me, he joined the immortals that day at Number Six. I would always have that memory of him holing out that birdie the last and most special round of our lives. The Lord knew what he was doing when he insisted that we take him with us that day. Dad and a nine iron had overcome the odds. He had finished in style and had made believers of all of us. Miracles do happen when you least expect them. That would have been in the late 1990's. He and mama won their battles and earned their wings in 2004. Both passed away in the bedroom they shared with Judy and me by their sides.

The Cuz Memorial Outing

In 2008, I had the opportunity to return to my roots, my hometown for a visit. My cousin, Sammy Cannon and his wife, Judy had invited us to the 100th Anniversary of the Abbeville Opera House, a black-tie affair saluting Vaudeville. Many Vaudevillian acts had appeared at the historical opera house in the 1900's. Abbeville is rich in history. I often forget that, after living there most of my life, just taking it for granted. I just never got caught up in the historic significance.

Cuz and his bride rolled out the welcome mat inviting us to stay with them for the weekend on beautiful Lake Greenwood just and a hop and skip from Abbeville. So, you ask, what does this have to do with whomping the ball; everything. What is a weekend without a little golf thrown in for good measure? We scheduled a golf outing for that Friday morning before the night's gala event at the beautiful Links at Stony Point golf course. Rounding out our foursome would be our old buddy Thumper and his cousin, both from the big city of Abbeville. Cuz is not a morning person, so he reserved us a 10:11 AM tee time, the course being less than fifteen minutes away. The skies were overcast with a chance of rain. It had already rained over three inches a couple of days before leaving the course ideal for a round. I love golf but I hate wet conditions. Wet is not my friend. Playing early in the south equates to dew saturated fairways often resembling a light rain shower. Not complaining, we were playing golf after all.

Observing standing puddles on his deck overlooking the lake, we realized it had rained during the night, another potentially bad omen. Cuz and I rendezvoused at the course with Thumper (Mike Culbreth) and his cousin who had gotten us the senior citizen discount rate. We were all of senior persuasion, so the rate was an accurate one. Wearing my golf knickers' ensemble, I certainly looked the part. Greenwood wasn't accustomed to seeing someone dressed like this. I did raise an eyebrow or two. I dress like Payne Stewart, may he rest in peace, but I definitely don't play like Payne. It just makes it easier on my partners, able to locate me when I'm in the woods looking for my ball.

The starter told us we had the course to ourselves. This is unheard of where I live on the Grand Strand for a mid morning tee time. Well, since the course was all inclusive just to us, we dubbed the event The Cuz Memorial Tournament. After all, we were all cousins, just not necessarily all related to each other. There would be no wagers because whompers don't bet. We know our limitations. There'd be no trophy, only pride on the line to not embarrass ourselves any more than usual. Wishing to play well doesn't always equate to executing the wish on the links.

Since we paid the old man rate, we figured it was only fitting to play from the yellow tees. To elevate our current status, we referred to this tee box as the Championship Tees, not the senior tees. It's all about perception and mental preparation. Mike 'Thumper' led us off on the first tee box. Oh yeah, we call him Thumper because he doesn't allow the ball to settle on the tee before he thumps the ground once then goes Happy Gilmore on the ball. We ended up giving him three do-overs on the first box until he finally long balled one down the middle. Practice makes perfect. Each of us required more than one drive to ensure we had a playable second shot. We exercised what is called the breakfast ball, a second shot if you prefer to take one on the first tee.

The wet fairways challenged our ability but our putting or lack thereof, took the real toll on the first nine holes. Cuz four putted the first three greens and three putted several of the others on the front nine. I too, experienced multiple putts but the wet turf is what really cursed my round, mentally taking me away from my game. Thumper's cousin had a roller coaster ride as well. Only Thumper prevailed, paring three of the first four holes, playing the best nine I had ever witnessed him play. He attributed it to having no adult beverages during the nine, a theory that would be questioned on the back nine.

At the turn, Cuz stocked up with a few cold adult beverages while Thumper stayed away from the temptation. The second nine bared no resemblance to the first. Cuz, able to leave his putting woes back on the front nine, overcame his phobia on the greens. Meanwhile, Thumper went into a tailspin, double paring two of the first three holes and never quite recouped from the bad back nine start. Cousin's game improved slightly from the first nine. I, too, turned my second nine around improving the back nine scoring by eight strokes and at least getting most shots off the tee box.

The most hilarious incident occurred when Thumper drove a tee shot about fifty yards off the box and into the awaiting Pampas grass. His ball set perched about six inches off the ground in the clutches of the grass. Thumper decided he'd play the shot. How did that go? Not too good! He whacked and wailed at the ball like a wild man trying to clear overgrowth with a swing blade. He did finally persevere, launching the ball back into the fairway. The event could have been worth ten grand if we had thought to video it and submit it to Funniest Home Videos. We did get some still photos as a reminder of his feat.

Thumper attempts to make that perfect pampas grass shot.

234

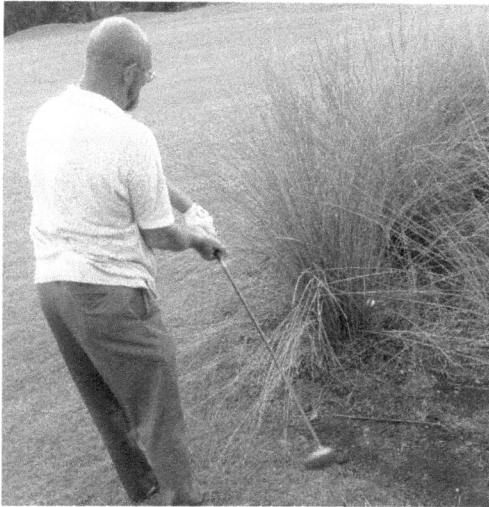

Trust me. This did not have a storybook ending.

You might recall that Mike was the one that went Tin Cup when we were playing on Punta Cana. He is also the bud along with Cuz that stood in the middle of the fairway chatting like they hadn't seen each other in ages while the group behind us fumed.

The final assessment of damages, Cuz squeaked out a marginal win with his back nine surge. Thumper hung on to second after his blow up. I finished four strokes back in third leaving cousin just a stroke behind me. We were all in triple figures. The first Cuz Memorial Golf Event had been dubbed a success.

That night we decked out in our tux and escorted our beautiful wives down the red carpet at the 100-year celebration of Abbeville's Opera House. I made the transformation from golf knickers to black tie and tails. We visited with old friends we had not seen in years. The entertainment included WC Fields and Mae West impersonators, the Abbot-Costello *Who's on First* routine, unicyclist, baton twirlers, a magician and many other acts. From whomping to walking the red carpet, the day had been exceptional. We consider ourselves fortunate.

Me and Cuz, My Brother

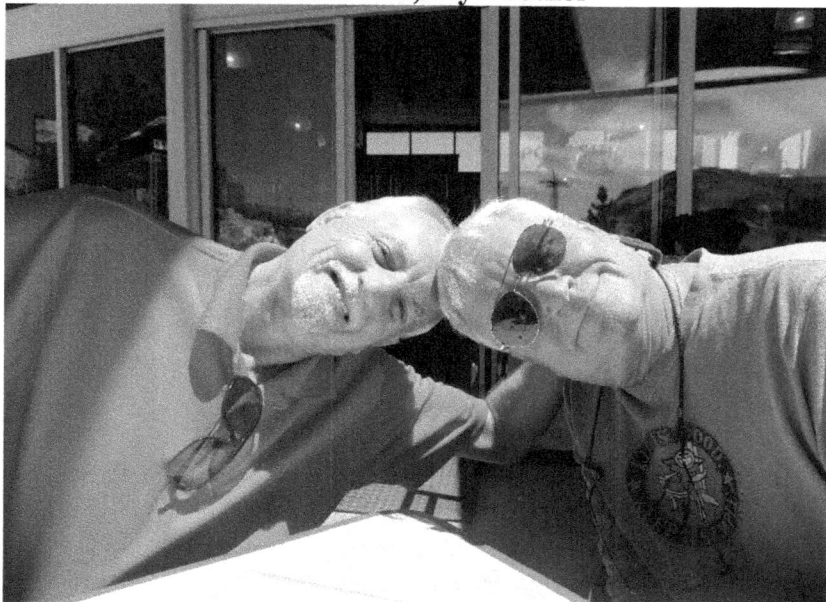

The 3rd Annual Cousins, In-laws, Outlaws and Branch Kin Golf Tournament

In 2010, the Hagens sponsored their 3rd Annual Cousins, In-laws, Outlaws and Branch Kin Golf Tournament in Anderson South Carolina at the Anderson Country Club. It would be a steamy, hotter than you know what, late July Saturday afternoon with temperatures and humidity testing the fortitude and stamina of the twenty-five brave golfers. I fall into the cousin category and this would be my first appearance at the event. I had just played in Conway, S.C. just days before with a heat index of 117 degrees. The temperature in Anderson felt like a cold wave in comparison. Sammy Cannon, Cuz, had invited me to the event. Let's clarify branch kin with this scenario. You and friend live along a creek. You live upstream and your friend lives downstream from you. You take liberty and pee in the creek. Your friend, oblivious to your outside habits, drinks water from the creek. He has now become your branch kin.

Arriving I was soon greeted by cousins of all shapes, sizes and ages, many of whom I had not seen in thirty or so years and others being offspring I had never met. Folks hailed from Pawley's Island and Myrtle Beach, South Carolina, North Augusta, Georgia and Charlotte, North Carolina to name a few. I'm certainly glad I had aged better than most of my kin but then again, they were staring at me and could have been thinking the same thing about my fifty-seven years of being rode hard and put up wet. Most everyone was already bleeding ignorant oil from every possible pore and we hadn't even hit the links yet. Southern boys know how to sweat. My Papa Bowie called sweating, ignorant oil, saying you might be showing your ignorance if you choose to work or play in the summer sunshine.

After the meet and greet session and after paying for my round at the Pro Shop desk, I reviewed the posted foursomes, eight teams strong. This would be a captain's choice format. My name just so happened to have two stars or asterisks beside it. I assumed this must acknowledge me as being the designated team captain, leading the charge for my team or it might identify me as a newbie to the fold.

After scrutinizing the other flagged names further, I determined I was wrong on both accounts. My bubble was quickly popped as these two little stars identified the one senior on each team. We old coots would be hitting from the yellow tees. At least I wasn't singled out. There was seven more of my kind on the roster.

Now for the record, I have no problem hitting from the yellow tees because that's my normal spot. As previously mentioned, we refer to them as the championship tees. It sounds better, right? Recognizing our elderly status seems a bit harsh. I think we could have sued and won if we had wanted to do so. I warned my younger cousin, Andy Hagen, who orchestrated of the tournament, that he too in just a few more years would be joining our ranks. Cuz said that we'd be super seniors by then and could move up to the lady's tee box. I, for one, am not shy about dressing for the part and becoming a trend setter if it moves me closer to the green.

Hydrating oneself is a serious matter in this sort of heat, so I brought my cooler of water. Others opted for beer and plenty of it. They missed something in translation and leaned more towards dehydrating themselves. Can you say *monkeying* on the fairways? My group drank moderately as compared to most of the other teams. This more than likely contributed to our scoring lower. Adult beverages plus extreme heat equates to cheap entertainment and distorted strategy in most cases, no pun intended with that case part.

My team consisted of two branch kin, Sloan, a local teenager, a foot shorter and one hundred pounds lighter than me. The kid might be the heir to the throne of a next generation of professional golfers. The others were Gerome, another long hitter from Charlotte and Tony, a cousin's cousin with as much grey hair as me but without the two stars by his name. We seemed like an unlikely foursome to contend but that tells you what I know about golf. When the dust had settled, we had posted a seven under par, good enough for first place and the cash prize. I had parlayed my five dollars into twenty-five and for the very first time in my life had won money playing golf. Did I flaunt it; only every chance I had. I did self appoint myself as Sloan's future agent. The kid could out drive and outplay everyone. I should have gotten him under a written contract.

My hosting cousin, Andy and his wife Joan, were way too gracious, offering an open bar and dinner at the club house on them for the twenty-five golfers and their wives and girl friends and family. Let's set the stage. Arriving at the 19th hole oasis are already intoxicated cousins, in-laws, outlaws and branch kin with free adult beverages of their choice at their fingertips. Is this going to get good or what? Break out the wading boots because this is going to get deep quickly. Tales, factual or fictitious, took on a life of their own. My cousins and their offspring are a step above when it comes to shooting the bull and throwing back one or twelve cold ones.

I asked some of my fellow double star patrons what was up with that one senior tee on number ten being behind the whites instead of thirty to eighty years up front. They had all noticed the unfair advantage, some selecting to move up to the whites. I stuck to the rules, stepped up to the yellow tee and launched one of my better drives of the day. I should have filed a protest at the club house though and demanded the resignation of the green's keeper and his entire staff, adding such injury to insult to us of the ancient class.

One of the cousin's fiancée needed a refill but couldn't obtain the attention of the bartender so Cuz stepped up to the plate and tapped his beer bottle on the bar, seemingly a fair gesture to alert the bartender that service was required. It got good ole boy's attention all right, a big behemoth of a bartender. He stepped over to the bar, finger pointed at Cuz, without any trace of a smile and in a tone that oozed of 'I'm only telling you this one time' he said, "I don't allow anybody to beat on my bar or whistle at me. I will not hesitate to throw you down the stairs and out of my bar. Do you understand?" Cuz understood as did the rest of us sitting on those stools. We were glad that Cuz had tested the uncharted waters first. We fully understood the ground rules moving forward. I think plenty of gents were saying, "Please may I have another, my good man?"

About thirty minutes later the big old bartender snuck up behind Cuz, grabbed him and planted a sloppy one on his cheek, saying he was kissing and making up. I think I would have rather had him throw me down those stairs. Cuz seemed almost relieved though.

While standing there the bartender said, "I don't have many rules for my bar. Banging on the bar and whistling are two. The third, I don't allow men in here wearing cowboy hats. If you come in my bar wearing a cowboy hat you best be riding a horse in here, then I'll serve you. Oh yeah, and women can wear sleeveless blouses providing they shave under their armpits. Now men, if you do shave under yours…" he winked and threw a little kiss.

Several asked me why I didn't wear my golf knickers to the outing. To that I replied, "Too hot", but I told them I would wear a pair and something argyle for them in a fall outing." Their words reeked of sarcasm, saying they wouldn't be caught dead in them. We manly men do not wear our emotions on our sleeves and are proud to be trend setters on the golf links. I thought but didn't say it, I might even wear my pink and black outfit next time and I for one know how to accessorize.

Deciding to leave the real partying to the professionals we, Cuz and our wives opted to make it an early night and said our farewell to the cousins, in-laws, outlaws and branch kin, which was no small feat. I think the entire process took over thirty minutes before we gained access to the exit. Cuz and I, eager to shower, unwind and kick back were highly disappointed after making the ten-minute drive to our hotel. We were greeted with a power outage, darkened and hot rooms with the hotel clerk unsure when power would be restored. Man, this was a fitting end to an already memorable day. We laid claim to an outside table with umbrella under sprinkling rain, with adult beverages and accompanied by our spouses, we waited for the power to be restored. Fortunately for us the power was back on within thirty minutes.

I for one can't wait until the 4th Annual Cousins, In-laws, Outlaws and Branch Kin tournament; my 2nd. I've secured my two-star spot on the roster and will be a defending champion. I have requested my same team, something everyone has told me will not happen next year. The only time I have ever won money playing golf and I can't get a break. Oh well, I suppose I will have to bring my saddle and spurs and ride someone else next time. At least I'm not branch kin.

As mentioned at the beginning of this piece, the 3rd event happened in 2010. And as also mentioned, Sammy Cannon, Cuz, lost his battle with Leukemia in 2018, February to be more specific. These events are always held the last Saturday in July and coincide with a family reunion on Sunday. I played in all but one of the next outings leading into the 10th, the July 2018 event. I had mixed emotions about playing in that one. It would be the first one since Sammy, Cuz, My Brother had passed. Sammy and I had never played in the same group for any of them but still, it would be the first without him. Wayne Paterson encouraged me to play, saying we would play with two of Sammy's playing partners to honor him. I had just published the tribute book, *Cuz, My Brother, Life is Good, God is Good*, and there would be friends and relatives present at the event who had reserved copies. I finally agreed that I would play and had been asked to say a few words about Sammy afterwards.

I thought of so many wonderful things to say about a man that I loved like a brother. This year's event would be honoring Sammy with photos posted in the clubhouse with a special Cuz golf towel for everyone playing. Just before we were about to have our after-golf meal, I was introduced to those gathered to share my memories of Cuz. I had a complete meltdown and sounded like a babbling fool. I stepped away and tried to compose myself and then tried a second time. I was too choked up to say a single word. Love hurts. Mourning the loss of Sammy continues to be a daily struggle. Over 150 family and friends reserved copies of the tribute book, a non-profit keepsake.

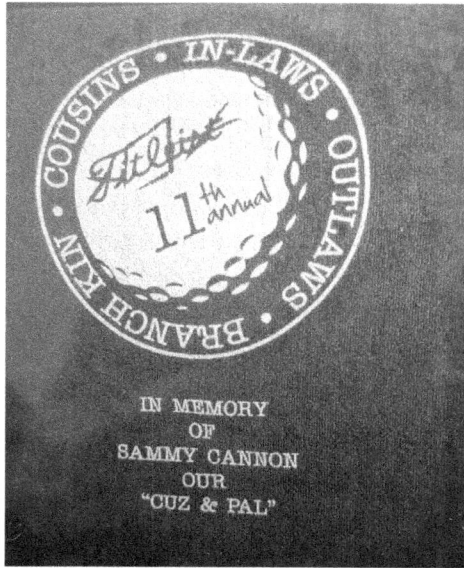

The Commemorative Golf Towel

Cover Photo for my book, 'Cuz, My Brother'

The Endless Mulligan
The Art of the Do-Over

Okay, you've read countless episodes with friend Carl (aka Bloody Carl) as the focal point. I've covered the method to his madness of utilizing mulligans or do-overs as he often refers to them once he has expended his supply of mulligans. Just anyone can't utilize the mulligan option as artfully as my dear friend. When the errant shot has been struck and almost before it has completed its wayward journey into the unfriendly abyss, popped up or traveled an unacceptable number of yards, his hand has already clutched the second ball in his pocket. After claiming 'mulligan' or 'do-over' he drops the ball in preparation for the redemption shot. Sometimes the second ball travels further and straighter than the first. Sometimes it doesn't. Not to worry, golf is a mere game and scoring is merely a mythical concept. The final validation of the round on the links is the tally recorded on the score card. It's not important how you got there, or the amount of extra shots taken. It's what you report to the score keeper that maintains a sense of sanity for the one struggling through the round. Ask Ken or Wayne. Each will support the premise and advance the narrative to protect their partner in crime.

It's not worth the time to tally your account of his scoring. Smiling and shaking my head, I just let it be. He's having an enjoyable round in most cases and it justifies his reason for returning for more. A score is but a score, right, wrong, exaggerated or fabricated. Golfers in general utilize the tools available to enhance their golf narrative. Foot wedges, *fluffing* of the ball on the turf, moving it here and there or intentionally unintentionally tallying incorrectly is part of the so-called gentleman's game. Mostly you'll only be called on it when wagering is involved or during tournament play. Just don't brag about a falsified score afterwards and claim you beat others if you really didn't. Scoring improprieties aren't worth losing a friend over. Carl is my brother and I cherish the brotherly bond. He and I became so close when Sammy, Cuz, my original brother was losing his battle with leukemia while Carl's dear friend Joe was losing his fight against cancer also. We learned to lean on each other when times were tough. Golf is but a game. Life is precious and friendship dear. God sometimes offers us a mulligan along the way.

The Lord offered me a wonderful mulligan when he allowed me to play that one last round with my daddy as he suffered through the dreadful disease, Alzheimer's. I saw daddy sink that birdie, the joy on daddy's face etched in my memory and my heart forever. Speaking of T.J, my dad; the Man above worked a couple of do-overs concerning him and my mama. I struggled as a 37-year-old man to come to terms with death as my papa's reign on earth ended at the age of 90. My mama had phoned me to tell me I needed to come to his home to see him one last time. I couldn't. I didn't because I couldn't bear the thoughts of him dying while I watched helplessly. Mama had a tough time forgiving me for that decision. Plus, neither my mama nor grandmother could understand why I didn't go to his bedside after he passed. I had my reasons. Not to fret, God utilized the endless mulligan making sure I was faithfully present for the deaths of my parents. I sat on the edge of mama's bed with her sitting beside me as she gasped her last breath, pancreatic cancer taking her. Her last words to me, "I love you sweetie." Daddy died three months later in the very same bedroom when he suffered aspiration while we fed him his pureed Sunday meal. The emergency responders didn't make it in time to resuscitate him. Then, my granny, 94 years old, died in her bedroom just six weeks after we relocated to the beach with her; one last mulligan, her passing in her bedroom at our home with us present. Her old body just quit working. My aunt told me that her time had come after she made sure I was happy after the move from Abbeville to Myrtle Beach. God had a plan even after I had disappointed my mama over my papa's death. The endless mulligan was executed when most needed.

The Lord wasn't finished yet. He has no shortage of mulligans in his bag. He opts to use them strategically I must add. When Sammy, Cuz, My Brother lost his battle with leukemia I was a broken man, devastated by the loss of man I loved like the brother I never had. God utilized His best mulligan to open my heart and use this do-over as a way for me to develop a relationship with Him. Sixty-four years old and finding the Lord for the first time was not a bad mulligan,

Big Guy, utilizing this grievous moment to push me into the pull. I'm still on that journey.

See, an endless mulligan can be the perfect option when played strategically. The Lord provides ample do-overs for those willing to accept them. Fore! Now begins the greatest game ever played. Amen…

In Cuz's words, 'Life is Good. God is Good.'

On the Wall of My Man Cave

Here are few throw-back photographs to the Flexible Technologies Days of the early 80's.

**Ricky (Bad Foot) Bryant, Me, Ronald Brock and Roddy Fleming
During Flexible Masters at Hickory Knob State Park**

**Harriet Simpson, Pat Thomas and Me
(Hickory Knob State Park)**

The Original Whomper at Hickory Knob

The Perfect Brand Golf Ball for My Game

About T. Allen Winn T. Allen

Winn began writing in 2003 while being cooped up in hotels during business travel. Completing a 650 page so called novel he became hooked. The homegrown Abbeville, S.C. boy embraced the experience completing one novel and then leaping into the next one, fun and therapy at the time. That changed in 2011 when a chance encounter brought stranger and new neighbor Bob O'Brien to his Pawley's Island doorsteps. Bob didn't realize the neighborhood home had been sold and apologized when Tom greeted him instead of the man he had expected to see. Book in hand, Bob had just published his first novel, The Toppled Pawn and explained the previous neighbor had shown interest in writing. Tom remarked he dabbled in writing to which Bob asked, do you have a manuscript? Tom replied ten. Bob had just started Prose Press, a publishing company and suggested publishing one. You can't make this stuff up.

T. Allen Winn's first novel, Road Rage joined the ranks of the published a few months later, and he owes a special thanks to Bob O'Brien for making this possible. His first seven books were published by Prose Press. In 2016, T. Allen Winn established Buttermilk Books, his publishing company. Ten books have now been published under Buttermilk Books. He and his wife reside in Myrtle Beach, South Carolina.

Ole T doesn't write under any specific genre. He writes what strikes his fancy. If you don't see something that fits your reading wheelhouse, just tell him what you like, and he might just write it for you.

Books are available on Amazon or online where books are sold. Select books are available at Southern Succotash on Washington Street in Abbeville, S.C. and in Tabor City, N.C. at Grapefull Sisters Vineyard. Or *Message* T. Allen Winn on Facebook to arrange delivery of signed copies.

Fiction from T. Allen Winn

The Detective Trudy Wagner series

Road Rage
North of the Border
Tithes and Offerings

Foot Series

Foot, Tree Knockers and Rock Throwers (1st in the trilogy)

More Fiction from T. Allen Winn

The Perfect Spook House
Dark Thirty
Lou Who
Raw Ride, a Wild West Zombie Apocalyptic Shoot'um Up
The Man Who Met the Mouse
Mister Twix Mystery, a Cat Scene Investigation

Non-Fiction from T. Allen Winn

Being Bentley, A Dog Like No Other
It's All About the 'A', Faith, Family, Football and Forever to Thee
with coauthor, Benji Greeson
It's All About the Angels in the Backfield, Dawn of a Dynasty
with coauthor, Benji Greeson
December's Darkest Day, While I Breathe, I Hope
The Hardwood Walker of Port Harrelson Road (based on true events
in Bucksport, S.C.)
Cuz, My Brother, Life is Good, God is Good

Memoirs

The Caregiver's Son, Outside the Window Looking In

Cornbread and Buttermilk, Good Ole Fashion Home Cooked
Nostalgic Nonsense
The Endless Mulligan, Short Shots from the Golf Whomper

Short Stories

For Your Amusement featured in Beach Author Network's book titled 'Shorts'

Ciled Me a Bar featured in friend and author, Danny Kuhn's Headline Book's
Mountain Mysts, Honorable Mention in Fiction at the 2015 London Book Festival and the book is endorsed by *Joyce Dewitt* of the sitcom *Three's Company*

Short story about Granny Bowie in friend and author Robert Sharpe's book, *The Heart and Soul of Caring*, about caregivers and their challenges

www.ingramcontent.com/pod-product-compliance
Lightning Source LLC
Chambersburg PA
CBHW060833110426
R18122100002BA/R181221PG42736CBX00040BA/1